1979

Α Β Γ Δ Ε Ζ Η Θ Ι Κ Λ Μ Ν Ξ Ο Π Ρ Σ Τ Υ Φ Χ Ψ Ω

ROYAL GREEK
PORTRAIT COINS

By
EDWARD T. NEWELL

Being an illustrated treatise on the portrait coins of the various kingdoms, and containing historical references to their coinages, mints, and rulers.

Published by

WHITMAN PUBLISHING COMPANY

Racine, Wisconsin

Originally Published 1937 by Wayte Raymond, Inc.

Α Β Γ Δ Ε Ζ Η Θ Ι Κ Λ Μ Ν Ξ Ο Π Ρ Σ Τ Υ Φ Χ Ψ Ω

No. 9090

TABLE OF CONTENTS

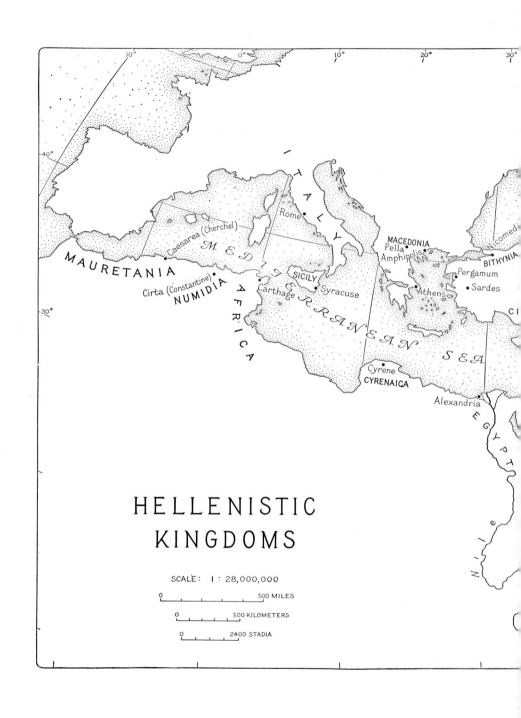

MAURETANIA

Caesarea (Cherchel)

Cirta (Constantine)
NUMIDIA

AFRICA

Carthage

SICILY
Syracuse

M E D I T E R R A N E A N   S E A

ITALY

Rome

MACEDONIA
Pella
Amphipolis

Athens

Pergamum
Sardes

BITHYNIA

Nicomed

Cyrene
CYRENAICA

Alexandria

EGYPT

Nile

HELLENISTIC
KINGDOMS

SCALE: 1 : 28,000,000

0   500 MILES

0   500 KILOMETERS

0   2400 STADIA

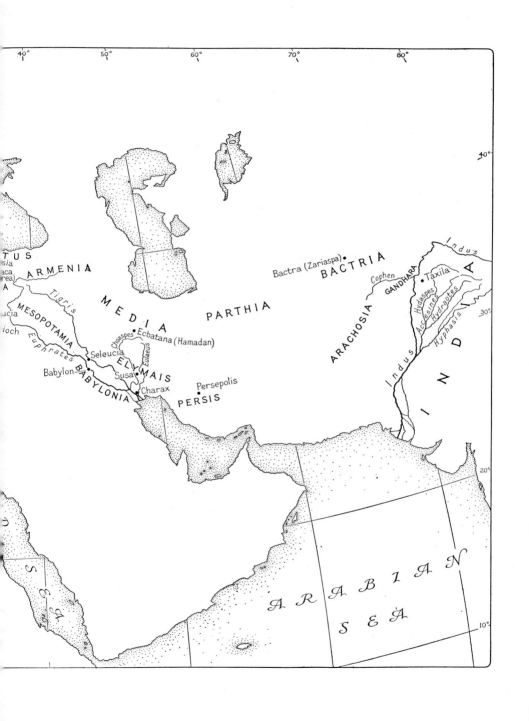

INTRODUCTION

THE peculiarly splendid portrait coinages of the Hellenistic monarchs are deservedly becoming more and more popular with collectors of ancient coins. These issues possess one outstanding characteristic which no autonomous coinage can hope to rival, and which renders the former of the utmost interest and importance to collectors, archaeologists and historians. They present us with an extraordinary series of living portraits — portraits of a quality such as only a Greek artist could produce. These men and women, be they famous or obscure, or even quite unknown to history, live again before our very eyes. Their several characters, their greatness and their foibles, grow tangible and real to us once more.

Nor should the at times artistically inferior reverses of these royal coinages be neglected. They frequently bear interesting allusions to contemporary events or to the ancestral origin of the dynasty. Or they give important representations of actual statues, or portray the ruler's favorite deity, or suggest his political aims and pretentions. They are sometimes commemorative, sometimes proclamatory. They frequently bear dates or regnal years, so that individual coins can be closely dated and so associated with the events which brought them forth or influenced the choice of their types.

This little book has not been produced with the advanced student or collector in mind; nor does it make any pretense at completeness. It is primarily intended to call the attention of collectors in general to the fascinating portrait coinages of the ancient kings, to indicate their great historic and artistic interest; to sketch in, very briefly, the political and historical background of both the coinages and their royal issuers. Almost without exception, it deals with the portrait coinages only, and especially with those in silver. Where no silver exist, or are particularly difficult to obtain, it may mention the gold coins or the more available copper. It commences with Philip of Macedon — the father of the Hellenistic Age — and his son Alexander the Great. It then describes the issues of Alexander's various generals and companions — the *Diadochoi* or

"Successors" *par excellence*. It then proceeds to describe, one by one, the portrait coinages of the many kingdoms which grew directly out of the fragments of Alexander's mighty empire. It closes with the royal issues of Syracuse, Numidia and Mauretania which, while never forming part of the empire, were never the less, historically and artistically, one with the later Hellenistic kingdoms.

Lest our volume become too bulky and forbidding, some limit had to be set. Hence the middle of the first Christian century has been somewhat arbitrarily chosen as the point at which to bring our little survey to a close. That date would comprise all the truly Greek issues. Thereafter such royal coinages as still continued have practically lost all Greek feeling and become purely Roman on the one hand, or purely oriental on the other. Even within our limits certain minor dynasties or princes have been omitted either because nothing is known of their history, or because their coins are negligible or so rare as to be practically unobtainable. Among the dynasts so omitted are the Bosporan kings and the Polemonian dynasty whose coins are far more Roman than they are Greek. We have also deemed it advisable, for various reasons, to pass over the petty rulers of Bithynia, Cilicia, Commagene, Trachonitis, Nabataea, etc.

Throughout, the writer has necessarily leaned heavily upon many well known historical works without its being possible to make due acknowledgment in each case. He therefore desires to express his grateful thanks for the extended use made of E. R. Bevan, "The House of Seleucus"; A. Bouché-Leclercq, "Histoire des Séleucides"; E. R. Bevan, "A History of Egypt under the Ptolemaic Dynasty"; Théodore Reinach, "Trois royaumes d'Asie Mineure"; such standard works as "The Cambridge Ancient History," Pauly-Wissowa, Smith's "Biographical Dictionary" and, last but not least, the inestimably valuable introductions to be found in the various volumes of the "Catalogue of Greek Coins in the British Museum."

EDWARD T. NEWELL

New York,

March — 1937.

ONE

THE COINAGE OF
PHILIP OF MACEDON

THE coinage of Philip II, father of Alexander the Great, is remarkable for several reasons. It was one of the earliest attempts in Europe at a bimetallic currency, and in its types and obviously planned arrangement it more nearly approaches our ideas of a national coinage than any other which the Greeks had as yet produced. Hitherto the issues of the little Greek city-states had been struck in the local mint and were also strictly local in choice of types, even though, in the cases of such active commercial centres as Athens, Aegina and Corinth, the money circulated extensively outside the narrow confines of the issuing city. Philip's coinage, from its very inception, was conceived on a far broader basis.

mint alone, but in several. Remarkable for Greece was the enormous extent of the gold coinage, at that time unrivalled by anything outside of Asia. Its commercial success was instantaneous and its types were copied for centuries afterward, at first in Asia Minor, later in Europe, particularly in Gaul, Britain and Germany. The silver tetradrachms, too, were extensively imitated, at first officially by mints in Macedonia under Alexander and his immediate successors, later by countless tribes residing in what is now Rumania, Bulgaria, Serbia, Hungary and Austria.

Posthumous Tetradrachm

Although several mints worked for Philip at one and the same time, it unfortunately never occurred to the mint officials to designate the localities of their particular mints. It apparently was deemed quite sufficient to mark the coins only with the private symbol or monogram of the responsible magistrate. Not only is this true of the coins actually struck under Philip himself, but also of the large posthumous issues which followed. Older scholars, making no distinction

Tetradrachm. Barbaric Copy

Beautiful heads of Apollo, Heracles, Zeus, and youthful hero appear on the obverses, while chariots, jockeys, horses, half-lions, weapons and symbols, even the mounted king himself as generalissimo of the national army, grace the respective reverses. This coinage was struck, not in one

between the contemporary and the posthumous coins bearing Philip's types, proceeded to assign this great mass of material to innumerable mints throughout Thrace, Macedonia, Thessaly and Greece proper, according as the symbols or monograms suggested the names or coats-of-arms of various Greek towns, villages and hamlets. Such a procedure is obviously mistaken, as it results in numerous instances of coins from greatly diverse dates and mints being found to have been struck from the same obverse die! Furthermore, Philip was by nature an organizer and consolidator. He most certainly would never have countenanced each little town of his wide realms striking money indiscriminately. Adequate supervision over such confusion would have proved well nigh impossible.

It therefore obviously behooves the student, first of all, to divide Philip's coins into two groups — the contemporaneous and the posthumous. The latter are rather easily distinguished by their later and poorer style, and more careless striking. Their symbols and monograms, too, are for the most part to be found on the coins of Alexander the Great, Philip III and their successors. For these kings, alongside of their own issues, also frequently coined with Philip II's types, because the latter's coins were still in great commercial demand.

The coins which were actually struck by Philip himself comprise about a third of the known gold varieties, about a third of the known silver, and practically all of the copper coins. We find gold staters, halves, fourths, eighths and twelfths; silver tetradrachms, didrachms, drachms,

tetrobols, triobols (hemidrachms) and diobols; and, finally, bronze coins in three sizes. By paying attention to style, sequence of dies, recutting of one magistrate's symbol over that of his predecessor, etc., the gold and silver coins fall readily into two great groups and several minor ones. The two large groups may certainly be assumed as representing the products of Philip's two largest cities — his capital at Pella and his most important commercial city Amphipolis. The latter, furthermore, was situated close to the rich gold and silver mines of Mt. Pangaeus and the surrounding districts. We may be sure that these two cities were throughout his reign the principal centres of coining. In addition, a series of gold staters, silver tetradrachms, drachms and hemidrachms, as well as copper coins, all with autonomous types and inscriptions (Obverse, head of Heracles; Reverse, tripod) were coined at Philippi.

Gold Stater Struck at Philippi

This city was a foundation of Philip, situated to command the famous gold mines of Crenides whence, it is stated, he drew as much as a thousand talents a year! No wonder that Philip's "dollar diplomacy" frequently proved more irresistible than even the prowess of his troops!

When Philip first came to power in 359 B.C. he did so as regent for his infant nephew Amyntas. But little Amyntas soon quietly disappears from history and the experienced, able, and ruthlessly ambitious Philip remains. His power, from the very commencement, rested upon his army which he soon brought to a perfection of discipline, military excellence and blind devotion to himself hardly ever before equalled in the ancient world. With such a leader at the head of such an army the remainder of Philip's career was an almost uninterrupted series of victories and conquests as district after district was added to his realm. Not the least important reason for his success lay in the almost inexhaustible gold and silver mines which he controlled, and in the quantity and excellence of the coins which he issued.

Tetradrachm. First Type

The earliest silver coins struck by Philip bear on their obverses a splendid and dignified representation of Olympian Zeus. On the accompanying reverses Philip himself is depicted astride a powerful war-horse advancing slowly to the left. The king is bearded and wears a military mantle and the national Macedonian cap or "Kausia." Obviously he is seen here in the guise of the Macedonian king, commander-in-chief of the army and the leader of his people. He raises his right arm in an impressive salute — the first representation on coins of what we now call the "Fascist salute." About 358 B.C. Philip secured Crenides and renamed the little mining town Philippi. He at once commenced to strike here the gold and silver coins mentioned above. Not long afterwards, either because Philippi was situated too far to the east or because its mint was not large enough to cope with the demands now being made upon it for gold specie, further series of gold issues were inaugurated at the more central mints, namely Pella and Amphipolis. For these issues the types

Gold Stater of Philip

chosen were the laureate Apollo head for the obverse, and the reverse, the galloping chariot in commemoration of the great victory which Philip had just won (357 B.C.) at the Olympian chariot races. The accompanying smaller gold denominations bore a head of Heracles, reputed ancestor of the Macedonian kings, with numerous reverse types such as half-lion, weapons of Heracles, or varying magistrate symbols. Such were the justly famous coins, popularly known as "Philippi," which quickly flooded Greece and brought down the price of gold, in terms of silver, from 12 : 1 to 10 : 1.

Tetradrachm of Finest Style

About 350 B.C. the reverse type of the silver tetradrachms was further changed. In the place of the mounted king we find the slim figure of a little jockey, holding the palm-branch of victory, riding a walking racehorse to the right. This type, too, is in direct allusion to a horse race won by Philip at Olympia — a victory of which he seems to have been inordinately proud. Likewise, the reverse types of all the small silver denominations and of all but the smallest of the bronze denominations similarly attest Philip's love of horses — as the meaning of his own name implies.

Such, then, was the first great royal coinage of the Hellenistic Age, an age usually considered to have commenced with Alexander but whose true foundation was certainly laid by Philip. In striking contrast to the narrow, prejudiced, "small-town" outlook of the earlier Greek communities, there now arose a more world wide, international tradition which reminds us so strongly of our own times. Quite commensurate with the "new age" and far horizons now dawning is the splendidly executed, well articulated and finely conceived coinage of Philip of Macedon.

THE COINAGE OF
ALEXANDER THE GREAT

PROBABLY no ancient Greek — be he hero, king or poet — is better or more widely known than Alexander the Great. His astounding overthrow of the mightiest empire up to his day, and the drastic political and economic changes which this entailed, have made a profound impression upon the world. Sober histories and imaginative fairy tales without number have been written around his deeds and adventures. Even today, perhaps more than ever, does his extraordinary success, the brilliance of his genius, the mysticism of his character, the breadth of his vision, the infallibility of his generalship intrigue both student and general reader.

Fortunately for the numismatist, the troubles which broke out in all parts of his empire the moment his able hand was removed by death caused innumerable hoards of his coins to be buried for safety's sake. As a result, these coins are now among the most common of all antiquity, and the collector of even the most modest means can gather a representative series so closely connected with one of the most extraordinary men of all times.

The way and the means had been well prepared by Alexander's father Philip II who, after subduing the remainder of Greece, was himself preparing the conquest of Asia Minor. His sudden assassination in 336 B.C. did, indeed, for a moment bring about a loosening of the bonds, accompanied by local uprisings and the threat of Barbarian invasions. But the young Alexander was quite equal to the task which had fallen so suddenly upon his shoulders. By military moves of lightning rapidity and brilliant conception he instantly met and conjured the appalling threats, until no man in all Greece durst question his power or his will. A general meeting of the Greek States was summoned to gather at Corinth in the spring of 334 B.C., and here Alexander with acclaim — some of it spontaneous enough, some of it induced by fear — was proclaimed leader of Hellas against the hereditary enemy, the Persian Empire.

Already had his father's trusted general Parmenio secured the crossing of the Dardanelles. Alexander with a veteran army of faithful Macedonians, aided by mercenaries and contingents from all the states of Greece, now invaded Asia Minor in what must have seemed to the world at large as something little short of hare-brained adventure. David could hardly have appeared more insignificant to Goliath than did the youthful Alexander with his scanty thirty thousand men and a depleted treasury did to the Persian colossus, ruler of all Asia from the Hellespont to India, master of millions of potential soldiery, owner of vast treasurers in gold, silver and precious stones. But Alexander was no fool, even if his temerity knew no equal. Well aware was he by experience that a small but well trained, veteran and devoted army, led by himself and his able generals, would prove more than a match against badly led hordes of divergent peoples and untrained levies. Little did he count the Persian treasures arrayed against his own meagre resources — were not these former there simply for the taking?

This is not the place to recount in detail our hero's numerous battles — each more successful than the last — his desperate sieges of well-nigh impregnable strongholds, his swift marches and distant campaigns, the consummate generalship and tireless energy which made them possible. One success led but to another; Persian army after Persian army was defeated, destroyed or scattered; city after city was stormed or forced to capitulate; province after province was traversed and subdued; the pusillanimous and vacillating Darius, as well as his ablest generals, were overwhelmed time and again — until finally Alexander stood on the banks of the Hyphasis in distant India, prepared to push on to the very ends of the world. But a great weariness, hardly surprising under the circumstances, at last overtook the army and it refused to go further. Alexander returned to Babylon, the world's metropolis and the proposed capital of his own empire. Here he immediately set about plans for consolidating his conquests, amalgamating the diverse peoples under his rule, welding together the great empire — but death, at the age of 32, overtook him and ended forever a career so gloriously begun.

From the very beginning, and soon confirmed by the Congress held at Corinth, Alexander always considered himself as the leader of the Hellenes against their hereditary enemies the Persians. In consequence, from the start, his coinages blazoned forth in their types this important aspect of his policy. The gold (double and single, half and quarter staters) bears the head of Athena, goddess of wisdom as well as of war, symbolic also of the superiority of Greek genius over Barbaric peoples. Perhaps especially to suggest Corinth, the seat of Alexander's panhellenic league against Persia, Athena wears the Corinthian type of helmet, usually adorned with her serpent. But not long after his earlier victories this serpent is frequently replaced by the eagle-headed or the more peculiarly Persian lion-headed griffin — both symbolic of the east which he was now conquering. Appropriately enough, the reverses of the gold coins display a beautiful figure of victory, at first standing, later gracefully advancing to the left and crowning his name with a wreath. Much of this gold was coined in Macedonia from the proceeds of the rich Pangaean mines, but more still was coined in the east from the bullion supplied by the immense treasures captured from the Persians.

The silver coins invariably bear the head of the youthful Heracles covered with the lion's skin — the features frequently resembling those of Alexander himself. The type proclaims Alexander's reputed descent from this the most popular of all Greek heroes, a dauntless protagonist and the conqueror of numerous fabulous monsters. How fitting a type for one starting out, as leader of the Greeks to struggle with the greatest empire of all the East! The accompanying reverses, for the most part, give us a dignified representation of the pan-hellenic god, par excellence, Olympian Zeus, enthroned and holding sceptre and eagle. Strictly Macedonian issues of the small denominations, however, replace Zeus with his bird the eagle. The copper coins, as well as some scarce hemiobols, bear on their reverses the weapons of Heracles, the club and bow in case.

It must be appreciated that Alexander was no mere conqueror, heedless of all but the enemy before him. He and his officials built as best they could, even while tirelessly pursuing the ever receding foe. As he advanced, mint after mint was put to work turning the captured Persian treasures into money for his own purposes. It was not necessary to erect new mints. The Persian empire had been well ordered, and composed of many flourishing and civilized communities where mints had often long been in existence. Alexander had but to instruct the officials in charge of these mints henceforth to turn out the new numerary. The actual workmen frequently remained the same as under the Persians. Thus is presented to the collector a fascinating picture of Alexander's advance, illustrated by one mint after another commencing to issue coinage in his name.

Tetradrachm. Pella mint.

In European Greece the principal mints of Philip II were continued by

Gold di-stater. Amphipolis mint.

Gold stater. Amphipolis mint.

Gold quarter-stater. Amphipolis mint.

Obol. Amphipolis mint.

Tetradrachm. Amphipolis mint.

Alexander, namely Pella and Amphipolis. Sometimes beautiful, their coins are usually more distinguished for the strength and boldness of their die cutting. They bear no mint marks beyond the symbols or monograms of the officiating magistrates. The moment Alexander set foot in Asia, and the distance separating him from his home base grew greater, additional mints were set in operation to keep not only his field army but also his garrisons, his commissary, and other rearward services supplied with cash. For this purpose, central mints which had functioned under the Persians

[17]

were usually selected. Thus, among other places, we find his money appearing at Lampsacus, chief city on

Tetradrachm. Lampsacus mint.

Gold stater. Miletus mint.

Tetradrachm. Tarsus mint.

the Hellespont and long an important coining center for gold staters; at Sardes, the capital of Lydia; at Miletus, chief city of southwestern Asia Minor, selected as a mint in the place of the partially destroyed Halicarnassus; and at Tarsus, capital of the province of Cilicia and southern terminus of the very important trade route northwards to the Black Sea. At first these issues, too, bore only magistrate's monograms or symbols, but the symbols have frequently a local connotation and the style and fabric of the coins themselves follow so closely the preceding Persian issues that their mints are not difficult to determine.

In Cyprus and Phoenicia Alexander found numerous city-states whose

rulers had long enjoyed the right of coinage under the Persian Empire. These rights were reconfirmed to those

Tetradrachm. Cyprus mint.

Tetradrachm. Citium mint.

Tetradrachm. Aradus mint.

Half obol. Sidon mint.

Tetradrachm. Damascus mint.

who submitted — but the types and weights were henceforth to be those of Alexander. Mint marks of local significance were employed for such issues; thus Salamis in Cyprus used the bow, while Paphos, Citium, Aradus, Byblus, and Sidon used monograms or letters. Tyre, because she refused submission and so had to be stormed after seven months of desperate siege, was partially destroyed, converted into a mere fortress, and deprived of coining rights. In her place, Ake (the modern St. Jean d'Acre) was granted the privilege of coinage. As this city had apparently possessed no mint previously, dies — and possibly die-cutters also — were transferred from Sidon for her first issue in Alexander's name. About this time another mint was likewise opened at Damascus, where large Persian treasures had been captured by Parmenio soon after the battle of Issus. These doubtless furnished the bullion for the new coinage, which was marked with the forepart of a ram, significant of the fact that Damascus was situated under the zodiacal sign of Aries.

Tetradrachm. Alexandria mint.

Alexander now proceeded to Egypt and, after securing that rich and flourishing province, founded there the famous city of Alexandria. It was not, however, until shortly before his death that a mint was opened, which struck perhaps the most beautiful of all his tetradrachms. These are marked with various symbols such as Head of the God Khnum, Thunderbolt, Rose, etc.

From Egypt Alexander moved forward to the last terrific and decisive battle with Darius, which took place on October 1st, 331 B.C., at Gaugamela near Arbela in Mesopotamia. The Persian army was destroyed, Da-

rius fled for his life across the mountains into Media, while Alexander

Didrachm. Babylon mint.

marched southwards and received the submission of Babylon, perhaps the most populous city in the world at that time. Here another important mint was opened which issued an immense series of coins, including the ever ostentatious decadrachm. Unlike the Cypriote and Phoenician mints, which were partially of a local nature, the Babylonian mint was a royal institution and of prime importance. Possibly for this reason its issues bore no special mint mark, except the symbols and monograms of the magistrates in charge.

With the acquisition of this vast metropolis our story practically ends. Alexander and his army swept on through Persia and India, completing the conquest of the Achaemenid empire. The great capitals of Susa, Persepolis, Ecbatana, Bactra, together with the fabulous treasures stored there, fell in succession to the Macedonian conqueror. But he seems himself never to have established mints in any of these places, though shortly after his death coins bearing his types commence to appear at Ecbatana and Susa. We have thus completed our hasty survey of the mints which he opened and the coinages which he inaugurated. The latter were destined to continue, practically unchanged, through several centuries. They constitute one of the most popular coinages of all times.

THREE

THE COINAGE OF
LYSIMACHUS

IT has been generally believed that Lysimachus was born at Macedonian Pella, but that his father originally came from Thessaly. Hence he was a Macedonian only by adoption, and this may account for the fact that, though six years older than Alexander, we hear little of him until he is mentioned as one of the king's personal bodyguard at the crossing of the Hydaspes in India. A little later he appears among the Trierarchs of the Indus fleet. Other than this, Lysimachus held no independent command under Alexander

The first mention in literature of Lysimachus is characteristic of the man. Quintus Curtius relates that when in 333-2 B.C., Alexander and his friends held a lion hunt in the royal park near Sidon, Lysimachus was attacked by an enormous lion, and though severely lacerated in the shoulder, he nevertheless, alone and unaided, overcame the raging beast. His undaunted courage and stubborn resolve was thus early indicated, and he later proudly commemorated the event upon his coins. A rushing lion, with spearhead below, alternates with the forepart of a lion and spearhead as the standard type of his copper issues — while the half-lion, again, is used as a personal symbol on many of his gold and silver coins.

Modern scholars are inclined to suppose that Lysimachus was really of good Macedonian stock, the tale of his foreign and rather lowly origin being put down to the derogatory propaganda of his many bitter enemies. Be that as it may, it is interesting to note that the other generals, in the division of the empire after Alexander's death, entrusted Lysimachus with the important but difficult governorship of Thrace. This province included the peninsula of the Chersonnese which commanded the Hellespont over which passes the land route between Asia and Europe, and so constituting the communications of the Macedonian armies in the East with their home land. It was also through the Hellespont that Attica and other large and populous districts of Greece proper drew their principal food supplies. Thus Lysimachus was charged with the holding of a most important and delicate position. Not only that, but the province itself was anything but pacified or subservient to Macedonian supremacy. The Greek cities (Abdera, Maronea, Aenus, Perinthus) which dotted its southern shores were of an independent nature, and probably ready to assert their former freedom at the earliest opportunity. Still more precarious was the Macedonian ascendancy over the wealthy Greek cities to the north, such as Byzantium, Mesembria, Odessus, Callatis, Tomi and Istrus. While as for the warlike Thracian tribes and kings of the interior, they were in open rebellion when Lysimachus arrived. Obviously the trust reposed in Lysimachus by his fellow generals speaks volumes for their faith in his ability, courage and integrity.

His first act was to face the bellicose Thracians. Though overwhelmingly outnumbered, Lysimachus yet managed to win a partial victory. Eventually he came to an understanding with the most powerful of his opponents, Seuthes, king of the Odryssae. By 313 B.C. his position in Thrace was largely consolidated, the while he adroitly avoided all entanglements in the internecine quarrels and wars of his fellow satraps. At this juncture, however, the cities of Callatis, Odessus and Istrus broke out in open revolt; Thracians and Scythians joined the rebellion; while Antigonus threw a small army under Pausanias into Thrace in Lysimachus' rear. The situation was desperate but Lysimachus rose magnificently to the occasion. With his usual boldness and energy he threw himself upon the Scythians and drove them out of the country; he captured Odessus and Istrus, and besieged Callatis. Leaving a small force here, he marched south, stormed the passes of the Haemus range held by Seuthes, surrounded Pausanias' army and forced it to surrender after the death of its commander. Callatis capitulated not long afterwards. In 311 B.C. a general peace was signed between the satraps, and Lysimachus was free to rehabilitate his province. Though war soon broke out again, Lysimachus kept himself aloof. In 308 B.C., near the site of Cardia, he founded a new capital and named it Lysimachia.

Throughout all this period Lysimachus had coined no money bearing his own types, contenting himself with the long accustomed coinage of the old Alexander types. The same is true

Tetradrachm of Alexander type

of the five peaceful years which followed the founding of Lysimachia.

In 303-2 B.C. broke out the final great struggle for the supremacy over Alexander's empire. On the one side were old Antigonus and his beloved son, that meteoric, unstable, incalculable genius, Demetrius Poliorcetes. Father and son, between them, dominated Syria, Asia Minor, a large part of the Greek mainland and the waters of the eastern Mediterranean. On the other side were the scattered but determined forces of Cassander of Macedon, Seleucus of Babylonia and Persia, Ptolemy of Egypt. Lysimachus, having once decided to join the coalition against Antigonus, acted with his accustomed boldness and energy. He suddenly threw his army across the Hellespont. Lampsacus, Parium and other cities opened their gates at once. Lysimachus swept through Mysia and Phrygia as far as the fortress of Synnada, which he captured. Another army, under his lieutenant Prepelaus, invaded Aeolis and Ionia, and even took the great city of Ephesus. Only when Antigonus himself arrived, having hastened northwards from Syria with practically all his army, was the advance checked. But the main object had been achieved, namely to force

Antigonus to concentrate the bulk of his field army against this dangerous thrust into the very heart of his empire. It was now the unenviable task of Lysimachus to hold him until the other allies arrived with overwhelming forces. With marvelous courage and steadiness he and his devoted army sustained repeated assaults, and, forced back by superior numbers, withdrew slowly northwards stubbornly contesting every inch of the way. Antigonus was thus held off until winter brought an end to the campaign. The contestants went into winter quarters, but Seleucus was now not far away.

The spring of 301 B.C. came, Lysimachus and Seleucus joined hands, the decisive battle took place on the plain of Ipsus. Antigonus fell, his army was scattered, his son Demetrius escaped to the sea coast where he sought refuge upon his fleet. The

Tetradrachm of finest style

Drachm of fine style

Gold stater

war was over and Lysimachus found himself master of Thrace and western Asia Minor.

Gold stater. Barbaric type

Lysimachus now inaugurated an extensive coinage in gold and silver at the mints of Lysimachia, Sestus, Abydus, Lampsacus, Alexandria Troas, Teos, Colophon, Sardes, Magnesia and elsewhere. The coins still bear Alexander's types but are all provided with Lysimachus' name and his personal badge, the forepart of a lion. These issues lasted a few years when, about 297 B.C., they were replaced by a new coinage of impressive beauty, simultaneously brought out in all the mints of the empire. The splendid, idealized head of the Hero Alexander, adorned with the ram's horn of Ammon, provides the obverse type. The reverse bears a well designed, beautifully executed figure of Athena seated to l., her left arm resting on a shield while with her outstretched right she holds a small winged victory who crowns the king's name with a laurel wreath. Gold staters, silver tetradrachms and drachms all bear the new types. The enormous quantities in which these coins were struck equally attest the commercial importance of their mints and the wealth and power of Lysimachus' empire.

As his power grew and his dominions extended, additional mints commenced to coin, such as Heraclea, Cius, Pergamum, Smyrna and others. When in 287 B.C., Lysimachus seized

Macedonia from the weakening grasp of Demetrius, the prolific mints of Pella and Amphipolis added their far from inconsiderable quota to the mass of Lysimachus' coinages. Probably no other of Alexander's immediate successors — with the possible exception of Ptolemy — issued money in such astounding quantities. No wonder that his somewhat ruefully jealous contemporaries dubbed Lysimachus the "Treasurer!"

His ambitions largely satisfied, fate willed it that the empire of Lysimachus should collapse even more quickly than it had arisen. Agathocles, the only son who was sufficiently capable to carry on the rule, had been executed in 284 B.C., through the machinations of his step-mother, Arsinoe, sister and later wife of Ptolemy II of Egypt. Rebellions broke out in Asia Minor, Lysimachus himself perished on the field of Corupedium, fighting against his old companion-in-arms, Seleucus; and his empire was divided between his rivals. His coin issues doubtless ceased at once — but their cessation was apparently very soon being painfully felt in commerce. Hence, almost immediately, numerous cities in the northern portions of his former empire commenced to take up again, and for their own account, the coining of his staters and tetradrachms. Thus we possess posthumous issues bearing the mint marks of Lysimachia, Aenus, Maronea, Perinthus, Cius and Calchedon. Over a hundred years later we still find such important commercial centers as Istrus, Tomi, Callatis, Byzantium, Calchedon, Heraclea, Tenedus, Rhodes and many others continuing to coin with the types of Lysimachus. For some time longer they thus served to keep alive the memory of that remarkable man, Lysimachus of Thrace.

FOUR

THE COINAGES OF
SELEUCUS I

SELEUCUS the Macedonian, sprung of sturdy country aristocracy, was of almost the same age as Alexander himself. A robust and athletic type, somewhat slow in thought, perhaps, but correspondingly courageous, ambitious, cautious and extraordinarily steadfast in purpose. Due to these characteristics his rise to power was a little slower than that of his rivals. He early became one of Alexander's very close companions, acquitted himself well of certain minor commands, was leader of the "infantry of the guard" at the battle of the Hydaspes, and after Alexander's death was appointed commander of the cavalry under the Regent Perdiccas.

In the revolt against the growing ambitions and pretensions of Perdiccas, Seleucus played a leading part; and in the ensuing division of the Empire at Triparadeisus in 321 B.C. he was rewarded with the Satrapy of Babylon. He had soon consolidated his province and endeared himself to his new subjects. This fact, coupled with his apparent ability and ambition, made him potentially dangerous to Antigonus who himself was now aspiring to the supreme power. By 316 B.C. Seleucus' position became so precarious that he was forced to flee from Babylon and sought refuge with Ptolemy in Egypt. Appointed commander-in-chief of the Egyptian fleet, Seleucus spent the next four years in harrying the coasts

of Antigonus' realms and finally, in 312 B.C., took a prominent part in the great battle of Gaza, where Ptolemy completely routed Demetrius Poliorcetes, son of Antigonus, and drove him out of Syria.

This was Seleucus' opportunity. With a handful of followers and a thousand soldiers lent him by Ptolemy, he made a dash through the enemy's country for Babylon. After facing countless dangers with great intrepidity and ability, Seleucus and his devoted band suddenly appeared before Babylon. His former subjects, remembering well his many benefits, received him with acclaim. Antigonus' garrison was overcome and Seleucus reigned once more in the great metropolis. The day of this astounding achievement, October 1st, 312 B.C., was ever afterwards celebrated by his descendants and from it is reckoned the well-known Seleucid Era, destined to remain in use for many centuries.

Antigonus could not allow Seleucus' bold stroke to go unchallenged. Not long afterwards Demetrius made an abortive attempt to recover Babylon for his father, but lack of time and the sturdy defense of one of the citadels of Babylon by Seleucus' followers, defeated his project and he retired baffled. Seleucus now gradually consolidated and increased his realm. In 306 B.C. he assumed the title of king. One by one he added the provinces of

Media, Persia, Bactria. When these had been securely amalgamated he invaded India to recover there the conquests of Alexander. But now he encountered unexpected resistance in the person of the great Chandragupta, king of Magadha, father of the still more famous Asoka, and founder of the mighty Maurya Empire. The two antagonists finally came to an agreement and Seleucus left India, taking with him as indemnity five hundred of the finest war elephants. With these he doubtless felt confident of being able successfully to meet his western rivals.

Hastening westwards he joined his ally Lysimachus, who in the summer of 301 B.C. was facing the might and wrath of Antigonus in northern Asia Minor. On the field of Ipsus the decisive battle was fought which ended in a complete victory for the allies. Antigonus fell and Demetrius fled for his life to Ephesus. The two old friends and companions-in-arms, Lysimachus and Seleucus, divided the Asiatic realms of Antigonus between them and Seleucus settled down to consolidate a mighty empire which stretched

Gold stater. Alexander type

Tetradrachm. Alexander type

from central Asia Minor to the borders of India.

Let us now turn to look at the coinages which accompany Seleucus' rise to power and which follow faithfully the ever widening frontiers of his possessions. During his first tenure of the Satrapy of Babylon he coined extensively in the name and with the types of Alexander the Great. Gold staters, silver tetradrachms, drachms and their divisions were issued in large quantities from the unusually important mint of Babylon, which supplied with money not only all Mesopotamia but also, to a great extent, the satrapies in the East. None of these coins bear any sign of Seleucus' power. Even after he had recovered Babylon in 312 B.C. no change, for a time, appeared in the types or inscriptions. When, however, in 306 B.C. he followed the examples set by his rivals and assumed the title of king, his name finally replaces that of Alexander, though leaving the types unchanged. Throughout the last quarter of the fourth century a special coinage, marked by the reverse type of a lion, and based on the old Persian weight system, had been issued from Babylon for special trade purposes. These "lion staters" (or tetradrachms weighing three Persian sigli) now bear, above the lion, Seleucus' personal emblem, the anchor.

As the empire of Seleucus spread, we find his name appearing on the Alexandrine issues of Ecbatana, Susa and other eastern mints. When the new capital of the empire was established at Seleucia-on-the-Tigris, the central mint was removed thither from Babylon. Here, then, were probably struck most of the coins which commemorate the Indian campaign: gold staters with Apollo head and Artemis in an elephant chariot; silver

Tetradrachm. Elephant quadriga

tetradrachms and drachms with Zeus head and fighting Athena in an elephant chariot. The Athena Promachus, consciously or unconsciously, may hark back to the reverse design of Ptolemy's current coins in the days when, for four years, Seleucus was the Egyptian king's most trusted admiral. Large though these particular silver issues may have been, the old Alexander type with the name of Seleucus still continued to be the standard coin of the kingdom and were issued down to the very end of his reign.

Tetradrachm with head of Seleucus

After the decisive victory of Ipsus, a brief coinage commemorating the event was brought out, in one or two mints only. On the obverse we see a somewhat idealized head of Seleucus himself, wearing a helmet adorned with panther's skin, bull's ears and horns, the latter emblematic of power and royalty. On the reverse is an attractive design of victory crowning a

trophy — not unlike, and possibly even suggested by, the reverse type of a contemporaneous western king, Agathocles of Syracuse.

Such, then, are the principal gold and silver issues of the great Seleucus, founder and master of a mighty empire. But one more type, as interesting and beautiful as it is rare, remains to be described.

In 281 B.C. large portions of the kingdom of Lysimachus rose in rebellion and called upon Seleucus for assistance. On the plain of Corupedium these two doughty Paladins — all that now survived of Alexander's immediate companions — met in final, titanic struggle for dominion over their hero's heritage. Lysimachus went down, fighting undaunted to the last. Seleucus remained, a lonely old man. A deep nostalgia seems now to have come over him and he hastened to cross the Hellespont in order to revisit his old Macedonian home from which he had set out with Alexander fifty-five years previously. But hardly had he set foot in Europe when he was struck down by an assassin's hand.

Tetradrachm with Indian elephant

During the brief interval between Corupedium and his death, a handsome coinage was inaugurated in his name, probably at Pergamum. On the obverse we see a spirited horse's head wearing the horns of power; on the re-

[26]

verse is one of the finest representations of an Indian elephant ever produced by a Greek engraver. The horse is surely the favorite steed of Seleucus himself, the noble animal which once by its speed and sagacity saved its master from imminent capture and to whose memory Seleucus is known to have erected a gilded statue just outside the gates of Antioch. The elephant of course typifies that dread contingent of the Seleucid army, brought from India and destined soon to be divided, some to become famous on the battlefields of southern Italy, others to save Seleucid Asia Minor from the Gauls. It might well be the pious wish of every numismatist that Seleucus' life had been spared a little longer — if only to make somewhat more available the beautiful coins of this final issue.

FIVE

THE COINAGES OF
PTOLEMY I

"PTOLEMY, son of Lagus, distinguished as an author, general, satrap and, later, king of Egypt" — so might have read a passage in some classical "Who's Who." Lagus himself probably belonged to the country nobility of Macedon. His son inherited a robust frame and vigorous mind; he possessed to a remarkable degree the shrewd caution, sound common sense, and genial nature which are so often characteristics of the best country stock. His mother, Arsinoe, may well have been related to the royal family — as the official geneology was later to claim. Certainly, as a boy, Ptolemy was a member of the corps of pages at the court of Philip II of Macedon. As such he became an intimate friend and playmate of the young Alexander with whom he grew up.

So soon as Ptolemy had proved his inherent military capacity during Alexander's expedition into Asia, he was employed on the most important occasions, became one of the seven personal bodyguards of the king, and signally distinguished himself in the Indian campaign. On Alexander's death Ptolemy's native shrewdness led him at once to foresee what was in store, and his equally well developed caution dictated his immediate steps. He early came to a secret understanding with Perdiccas, Regent of the Empire for Alexander's heirs. He backed Perdiccas at the great council of the chieftains held in Babylon, and in turn was rewarded with the satrapy of Egypt, which he had recognized as the safest and most promising province of the entire empire. Wasting no time, Ptolemy immediately departed for his chosen satrapy, and once within the Egyptian frontier set about establishing a firm foundation to his power.

In the meanwhile, Alexander's body was being borne westwards from Babylon in magnificent state — eventually to repose, as Perdiccas had arranged, among the tombs of the Macedonian kings at Aegae in Macedon. But Ptolemy fully appreciated the immense prestige which would accrue to himself and to his adopted country in the possession of the great hero's body. While Perdiccas was absent, campaigning in central Cappadocia, Ptolemy led his army to meet the funeral cortège, proceeding through Syria to the sea, and diverted it to Egypt. The body was temporarily placed in the sacred city of Memphis, ancient capital of Pharaonic Egypt, — but Perdiccas had become Ptolemy's bitterest enemy.

Ptolemy's next step was to annex the Cyrenaica, which would serve admirably as a bastion on the west and from whence he could draw Greek soldiery for his army. But now Perdiccas, in the spring of 321 B.C., at the head of the entire royal army, advanced upon the rebellious satrap. This great army, which had conquered half of Asia, shattered itself in vain against the desert defenses, the swamps and lakes, the interlacing canals and eastern arms of the Nile which together constituted Egypt's impregnable eastern bulwark. The defeated army rebelled, Perdiccas was assassinated, and the Macedonian chiefs met at Triparadeisus in Syria to partition the empire anew. The successful Ptolemy was offered the Regency but chose the wisest and safest course, and merely had himself confirmed in the possession of Egypt and Cyrene. The ancients, in fact, likened him to a tortoise who would from time to time reach forth to secure what he desired, but who always had a safe retreat into which he could withdraw whenever serious danger threatened.

bols of the magistrates responsible for the coinage. About 320 B.C. Ptolemy showed his initiative and independence by being the first of his fellow satraps to alter the type of his silver coinage. The seated Zeus, even the accompanying name of Alexander on the reverse was indeed left unchanged — but the head of Heracles was replaced by a more obvious portrait of the great Alexander himself, covered with an elephant's skin headdress. This new type not only suggested the hero's famous conquest of distant India (incidentally the scene of Ptolemy's own most outstanding military exploits), but also reminded the beholder of Egypt's possession of Alexander's body. For to the ancients the elephant (the royal beast, par excellence, the most intelligent and powerful of all the animal kingdom) always connoted something of royalty and divine apotheosis. Thus, even in Roman times, the elephant-drawn chariot or funeral car was used as a favorite type on coins struck in memory of a deified emperor.

Down to this point Egypt had been merely a province of Alexander's empire. The mint established at Alexandria had been striking gold staters and silver tetradrachms bearing the accustomed types of Alexander the Great, and so were indistinguishable from the remainder of his money, except by style and the accessory sym-

Between 320 and 318 B.C. Ptolemy was sufficiently emboldened by the growing dissension among his rivals to reach out and secure the important district of Palestine. Somewhat later, to conform with his increasing ambition and his plans for the future, the reverse type of the silver coinage was changed. The head of Alexander in the elephant skin remains, but the seated Zeus gives way to a splendid figure of the fighting Athena. On the first issue of this new type we read the inscription: ΑΛΕΞΑΝΔΡΕΙΟΝ ΠΤΟΛΕ-ΜΑΙΟΥ i. e."The Alexander (tetradrachm) of Ptolemy." The succeeding issues revert to the simple ΑΛΕΞΑΝΔΡΟΥ once more. Thus Ptolemy not only precedes any of his fellow satraps, by some ten years, in placing his own name on a coin, but also proclaims the fact that this is his own type of the Alexander money, presumably planned to take the place of the old coinage.

Shortly afterwards Cyprus was acquired, because of its importance as a naval base and because of its much needed supplies of ship's timber, pitch and copper mines. Ptolemy was evidently aiming at the naval hegemony of the Greek world. It also seemed important to him to play in with Rhodes, whose merchant princes practically held the financial primacy of the Aegean, and so he soon changed the weight standard of his silver coinage from the Attic to the Rhodian. His tetradrachms, which hitherto had weighed a little over seventeen grammes, henceforth weigh about fifteen and a half grammes — though the types remain unchanged.

Egypt's rapidly growing power was obviously a dangerous menace to Antigonus' own plans for world dominion. The latter's powerful army was set in motion against the Egyptian forces garrisoning Palestine. Before the advancing might of Antigonus, Ptolemy discreetly withdrew behind his now famous desert defenses. In 312 B.C. the latter essayed a lightning thrust against Palestine, routing Antigonus' son Demetrius at the memorable battle of Gaza. But Antigonus soon moved south to retrieve the disaster, and within three months Ptolemy was back within his shell once more. In 307 B.C. his rival decided to crush him, once and for all. Demetrius suddenly descended upon Cyprus, utterly routed Ptolemy and his fleet and captured the island itself, together with Ptolemy's brother Menelaus and his army of nearly twenty thousand men. Father and son then joined hands and with their combined forces advanced upon Egypt by land and sea. Once more the eastward defenses of Egypt held firm; Antigonus retired completely baffled, his army shaken and his son's fleet all but destroyed.

Ptolemy thereupon followed the example set by Antigonus, Demetrius, Seleucus and Lysimachus, and formally assumed the title of king. To commemorate the event he finally abandoned Alexander's types for his gold staters, placing instead, his own diademed portrait (the first of all the "Successors") on the obverse, while on the reverse we see the divine Alexander, holding the thunderbolt of his "father" Zeus and standing in a chariot drawn by four elephants.

Four years later Ptolemy joined the coalition of princes formed to crush Antigonus. Father and son were at the head of their armies in Asia Minor to meet the combined forces of Cassander, Lysimachus and Seleucus. Ptolemy seized this opportunity to invade Palestine once more. To be sure, he hastily retreated on receiving the false news of a victory by Antigonus — but returned immediately when the rumor proved to be unfounded. The decisive battle in the north was fought in the summer of 301 B.C. at Ipsus, where Antigonus and his empire perished. As a consequence Ptolemy settled himself firmly in Palestine, Coele-Syria and southern Phoenicia. From the weakening grasp of Demetrius he eventually wrested the flourishing seaports of Sidon and Tyre, as also the vastly important island of Cyprus. His kingdom, or perhaps rather empire, was now well rounded out and definitely established.

Because of the new conditions, a complete change in both types and standard was now effected in the Egyptian coinage. The age-old Phoenician weight system was adopted. A splendid series of coins in all metals was issued, embracing gold pentadrachms (actually called "trichrysoi" or triple staters by the Alexandrians) and obols, silver octadrachms, tetra-drachms and rare drachms, together with several denominations in copper. On the obverses of all gold and silver pieces we behold a finely executed and most realistic, diademed portrait of Ptolemy himself. Of this work the artist is justly proud and signs with the initial of his name, placing the microscopic letter delta behind the king's ear. The reverse type is a proud and splendid eagle, defiantly facing to the left and clutching the thunder-bolt in his wicked looking talons — a truly noble beast, destined to be copied again and again by admiring die-cutters on the coins of Nabataea, Tyre, Sidon, the Seleucid kings, Elis, Sparta, Epirus, Tarentum, the Bruttians, Syracuse, Agrigentum, Capua, Rome — and countless other mints throughout succeeding centuries.

As a permanent coinage, the tetra-drachm continued practically unaltered, to the very end of the dynasty; down, in fact, to the autumn of 30 B.C. when Ptolemy's equally famous descendant, Cleopatra, employed the poisonous asp to cheat Augustus of the ultimate completeness of his triumph.

SIX

THE COINAGES OF
DEMETRIUS POLIORCETES

OF all Alexander's immediate successors the most vivid personality and most stirring story is that of Deme-

Gold Stater of Demetrius

trius, "Besieger of Cities." There was no height of glory or depth of despair that was not experienced — not once but many times — by this extraordinary man in the course of his remarkable career. And his coinages are no less varied and interesting than the history of the man himself.

During the lifetime of his able and indulgent father, old Antigonus Monopthalmos ("he of the single eye"), Demetrius struck no coins of his own, although he was his father's right hand, commander of his powerful fleet, leader of many expeditions and campaigns in Greece, in Palestine, in Cyprus, in Babylonia, against Rhodes and along the Hellespont. Finally, in 301 B.C., came the great coalition of the other rulers against the much feared Antigonus. It culminated in the mighty battle of Ipsus which left Antigonus a corpse on the battlefield, Demetrius a fugitive, their empire shattered and their army destroyed. Demetrius succeeded in escaping to Ephesus where lay his fleet. Knowing that all was temporarily lost for him in Asia, he proceeded to Athens, in

order to save at least his Grecian possessions. But now he made the bitter discovery that the fickle Greeks would have none of a defeated ruler and were already in open revolt.

In his extremity, Demetrius with his fleet turned once more to the East, where he still retained hold of a few strong places, such as Ephesus, Miletus, Caunus, Cyprus, Sidon and Tyre. Cyprus especially was his mainstay and an ideal vantage point from which to recoup his shattered fortunes. Here lay the powerful fortress of Salamis, Demetrius' naval base and the scene of one of his greatest triumphs. Seven years previously, with inferior forces, he had captured the island from Ptolemy and had defeated the Egyptian king off Salamis in one of the hardest fought and most decisive naval engagements of all times.

At this juncture the "bright-eyed Goddess of Fortune" gave the lie to her usual reputation and proved more constant than Hellenic subjects. Seleucus made overtures of peace, suggested an alliance and requested the hand of Demetrius' daughter, Stratonice. Demetrius at once sailed for Syria. Skirting on his way the Cilician coast he there staged one of the boldest and most lucrative raids in history. In the little hill fortress of Kynda there still lay what remained of the immense treasure which Alexander was in the process of forwarding home to Macedonia when he died.

From time to time his successors had dipped into this treasure for purposes of their own. At this moment, however, there still existed some twelve hundred talents — a matter of over a million and a half of our present dollars, with a far higher purchasing power. This, Demetrius now seized from under the very nose of its outraged guardian, Pleistarchus,—brother of Cassander and at this time ruler of Cilicia. This much history records. It is an obvious deduction that Demetrius must at once have forwarded this bullion for safety to his nearest stronghold, Salamis, which lay almost within sight of the Cilician coast. Here, in a mint of long standing, it was turned into coin. These coins have come down to us in considerable numbers and constitute one of the most beautiful and interesting issues of all the successors.

Figure 1.

On the obverse (Fig. 1) we see the winged Goddess of Victory, blowing her trumpet and descending upon one of Ptolemy's defeated war-ships. In this choice of type Demetrius was harking back to perhaps the most glorious moment of his entire career. He chose the type not solely in a boastful spirit, but with the distinct purpose of impressing upon friend and foe alike that he was still the greatest living sea-captain of his age and that he and his invincible fleet remained the domi-

nant sea power in the eastern Mediterranean. The reverse, too, accentuates Demetrius' claim, for here we behold Poseidon, God of the Sea, striding across the field in fighting attitude and belligerently brandishing his trident. Such types are definitely propaganda and chosen for the purpose. The beautiful figure of victory was probably copied from a statue (by the famous sculptor Eutychides) erected by Demetrius in commemoration of his great victory. It is this very statue, or a later Rhodian version, widely known as the "winged victory of Samothrace" which is one of the glories of the Louvre and familiar to every tourist visitor to Paris.

The loot of Kyinda was large, but so were Demetrius' financial needs. Tetradrachms of the Victory type were struck in quantities at Salamis, and they also appear at other mints — such as Ephesus, Miletus and, eventually Tarsus, after its capture from Pleistarchus. At Tyre, however, the old Alexander type was still continued but now the name of Demetrius replaces that of the long dead Alexander.

The year 296 B.C. finds Demetrius again in Greece, striving to rebuild his lost dominion there, campaigning and besieging cities. Whilst thus engaged a renewed coalition of Lysimachus, Seleucus and Ptolemy suddenly seized practically all that remained of his Asiatic possessions. After this portentous frown, Dame Fortune became contrite and soon smiled again upon her favorite. Cassander having died in 297 B.C., his eldest son succeeded, but only for a brief space. On the latter's demise the two remaining sons soon became embroiled in a fratricidal struggle for supremacy. Demetrius seized the opportunity to intervene in Macedon and appropriated their patrimony for himself. Thus, at one stroke and with little trouble, he had gained more in Europe than he had lost in Asia. Among other things which he thus acquired were the two active mints of Pella and Amphipolis, together with the still vastly rich gold and silver mines of Philippi and Mt. Pangaeus. At once silver tetradrachms of the Victory type, as well as gold staters of the usual Alexander type (but bearing Demetrius' own name), were struck at these mints.

Figure 2.

In 292 B.C. completely new types replace the old. We now find (Fig. 2) the diademed, horned, portrait head of Demetrius himself on the obverse. This sudden and radical departure from long established custom is but what one might have expected in a man of Demetrius' proud, bold and hasty character. In all the continent of Europe he was the first ruler to dare thus openly to place his portrait upon the coinage. The reverse type of the new coins depicts Poseidon seated upon a throne of rocks, holding a trident and an aplustre (the stern-ornament on an ancient Greek war-ship). Soon the reverse type is again altered (Fig. 3) and Poseidon is seen erect, his right foot placed upon a rock, his left hand resting upon the trident. The

god appears to be gazing out to sea, surveying the rocky promontories

Figure 3.

and restless waves which constituted Demetrius' real dominions.

In enormous quantities the above coins were issued from the central mints of Pella and Amphipolis, together with subsidiary mints in Macedon, Thessaly and Greece proper — such as Demetrias, Thebes and Chalcis. For Demetrius was now preparing a mighty armada with which to attack his rivals in a bold bid for supreme dominion over all of Alexander's former empire. The navy yards and arsenals of Pella, Demetrias and Chalcis seethed with feverish activity, troops were assembling and recruits were drilling everywhere. The resultant call upon the cash reserves must have been stupendous, and the coins that have come down to us attest by their numbers the attempt to meet the demands.

At this supreme moment, however, Demetrius' fortune finally and definitely deserted him. The weary populations of Macedonia and Greece rebelled against further military adventures, with their concomitant wars, poverty and misery. Macedonia and Thessaly went over to Pyrrhus, most of the Greek cities fell away, and Demetrius found himself once more master only of a fleet. Though practically bereft of power, Demetrius refused to abandon the idea which had obsessed him. With what was left to him of followers he made an attack upon Asia Minor in one last desperate bid for power. In spite of a few initial successes, the armies of Lysimachus, under the able leadership of Agathocles, eventually maneuvered Demetrius out of city after city and away from the sea which represented his only real power. All across Asia Minor Demetrius led his harried and ever dwindling forces, eventually crossing the Taurus Mountains and so into the arms of the waiting Seleucus. The ensuing engagements reduced his weary forces to a mere handful of still faithful followers — and the game was up. Demetrius was persuaded to throw himself upon the mercy of Seleucus. He was placed in honorable but safe captivity on a royal estate near Apamea in Syria. His proud and restless spirit, however, could ill brook such restraint and ere long he had drunk himself to death.

Thus ended one of the most extraordinary of men. His coins still remain to illustrate by their many and varied mints, types and issues, the fascinating story of the brilliant but unstable genius that was Demetrius the Besieger.

SEVEN

THE LAST KINGS
OF MACEDON

NO true portrait coins of the Macedonian successors of Demetrius Poliorcetes appear to have been issued until the reign of Philip V. Philip was the son of Demetrius II and grandson of Antogonus Gonatas. On the death of his father in 229 B.C., when Philip himself was only eight years old, the regency was assumed by his uncle Antigonus Doson. In 220 B.C. Doson died and Philip, now a young man of seventeen, came to the throne.

During the first three years of his reign he was engaged in a war with the Aetolians who by their fighting qualities had played a large, often a preponderant part in Greek affairs. Although nearly all the remaining states of Greece were allies of Macedon in this conflict, the support which they furnished was but feeble and the brunt of the war devolved upon the young, able and energetic Philip and his veteran Macedonian troops. Considerable success crowned his efforts, but both sides grew equally weary of the indecisive conflict, and peace was eventually signed at Naupactus in 217 B.C.

No small contributory urge toward peace was furnished by the terrific struggle between Rome and Carthage at this time raging in Spain and throughout the Italian peninsula. Instinctively the Greeks well knew that the outcome was bound to have great effect upon their own future. As Macedonia and Greece had less to fear from a successful Carthage than from Rome, Philip in 215 B.C. concluded an alliance with Hannibal. Philip made leisurely preparation for the war with Rome, met with some ill success before Apollonia but carried on a more successful campaign against the Illyrian tribes, and thus continued to postpone any active intervention in Italy itself. Probably he was expecting the two great antagonists to annihilate each other, to his own considerable advantage. Rome, however, preferred to take no chances with a potential Macedonian foe and so set about furnishing Philip with enough trouble to keep him at home. She allied herself with the Illyrians and, soon after, with the Aetolians and so, through them, started a war at Philip's own doorstep. Many of the Greek states, some willingly, some perforce, sided with the Aetolians, and Philip found himself in a complicated and rather painful situation. All of his best qualities now came to the fore and he fought this war with energy and ability. He gained some successes over the Aetolians and their allies who soon found that Rome was in no position to send them much real assistance. Eventually in 205 B.C. a temporary peace was patched up, thus allowing Rome complete freedom to settle finally with Carthage.

It must have been at some period during these early years of his reign, while military success still crowned his arms, that Philip issued his first series of portrait tetradrachms (Fig. 1). On the obverse is a very spirited head of the young king, bearded and wearing a diadem with fluttering, fringed

Figure 1.

ends. On the reverse the warrior goddess Athena strides to the left, her star-adorned shield held out before her, her right hand raised, brandishing a thunderbolt.

Philip now turned eastwards in a search for easier military laurels and increased territory, and embarked upon an adventurous campaign in Asia Minor. While he was meeting with considerable success, but accompanied by some misfortune, the great battle of Zama brought the Second Punic War to a definite conclusion. In 200 B.C. Philip was forced to return to Europe in great haste, for Rome had decided to settle scores with the Macedonian king and had suddenly declared war. The new conflict dragged on with varying fortunes until 197 B.C. when T. Quinctius Flamininus assumed command of the Roman armies in Greece. He brought the war to a swift end by winning the decisive battle of Cynocephalae. Philip sued for peace, was forced to give up all his conquests together with his entire fleet, to reduce his army to five thousand men and to pay an indemnity of a thousand talents.

Philip was for the time being hum-

bled and resigned to his fate. He abided loyally by the terms of the peace treaty and aided the Romans in their wars with the Aetolians and with Antiochus III. In return, Rome treated him rather cavalierly and forced him to surrender such towns as he had secured while her ally in the above mentioned wars. Bitterly disillusioned and filled with renewed hate for the she-wolf's brood, he prepared steadily, 187/6 to the day of his death in 179 B.C., for the coming war.

Figure 2.

Figure 3.

No small part of this preparation consisted in a systematic exploitation of the Macedonian silver mines, and a concomitant steady production of coined money. A very handsome series of tetradrachms (Fig. 2), didrachms (Fig. 3), drachms and hemidrachms is the result. As the obverse type of the largest denomination we have a Macedonian shield, its boss ornamented with a bearded portrait of Philip in the guise of the hero Perseus, with winged, dragon-headed helmet and the usual harpa. The reverse type on all denominations is the club of Heracles surrounded by an oak wreath.

The obverse type of the smaller denominations is a fine, though sometimes a rather brutally depicted, diademed head of Philip facing to right. The coinage lasted seven years, and we find that the several issues are each marked with its special symbol such as harpa, club, caduceus, thunderbolt, tripod, trident and star, all placed outside the wreath.

When Philip's son Perseus ascended the throne in 179 B.C. he inherited his father's hatred of Rome, and the now well advanced preparations for a great war. The following years were spent in still further strengthening his army and finances, in securing the good will of the various Greek states and in acquiring useful allies.

Figure 4.

The extensive silver coinage inaugurated by his father was continued by Perseus. The initial issue of tetradrachms (Fig. 4) displays a finely executed portrait, but one whose features bear far more resemblance to Philip than they do to Perseus. On political grounds this close resemblance may actually have been intentional. For, according to both Livy and Plutarch, rumors were widely circulated not only that Perseus had sprung from a morganatic marriage but that he was even a changeling and not Philip's own son. In any case, as these coins are so beautifully cut, and are further

distinguished by bearing the name ΖΩΙΛΟΥ in full beneath the king's neck, it would seem that we have here an

Figure 5.

artist's signature — as has been frequently suggested. These coins may therefore be looked upon as having something of a medallic or commemorative nature, being struck in the first days of the new reign. The immediately succeeding issues are also particularly fine (Fig. 5), though they do not bear a signature on their obverses. The portrait appearing on these coins is obviously that of Perseus himself: very handsome, but with a sharper, more protruding nose, a more sloping profile and less tightly curled locks than those possessed by Philip. The reverse type of all displays an eagle, with open wings, standing proudly to r. upon a thunderbolt, the whole design being enclosed within an oak wreath. On the initial issue mentioned above, the eagle is larger and particularly well designed, and the oak wreath is so carefully and minutely drawn that we can even see the acorns depicted here and there. Accompanying didrachms and drachms are also known, but these denominations are very rare. Instead of the eagle they have for their reverse types, respectively, a harpa or a club encircled by an oak wreath.

A person of attractive manners, a

fine and handsome figure, a noble carriage, trained by his father in the arts of war yet quite free from the latter's dark strain of uncontrollable temper, suspicion, treachery and other low propensities, Perseus seemed a man destined to play a splendid role. With great ability and statesmanship he laid his plans and prepared successfully to defy even unconquerable Rome. But now, certain grave faults in his character made their appearance and brought utter ruin upon himself and his country. He lacked boldness, and the unfaltering determination to win through. At the last moment he hesitated, his courage deserted him, and he tried to evade, or at least to postpone, the inevitable war which Rome herself had now decided to bring about before it was too late. While Perseus vacillated, Rome acted. While he was sending a futile mission to Rome, she worked behind his back and, diplomatically and otherwise, deprived him of all his friends and allies. Then she declared war, but the conflict dragged along for three years, due to the incapacity of the Roman commanders and Perseus' desire to stand only upon the defensive. In spite of this he was actually victorious in two major engagements but failed completely to take advantage of his success. When a touch of boldness and the slightest evidence of real military ability would have aligned all Greece and Asia behind him, he feebly retired within the Macedonian frontier to meet the enemy's onslaughts there. To cap all, his inherent stinginess now asserted itself and, in spite of the immense supplies of precious metals stored up so laboriously by his father and himself, he docked

his soldiers' pay, lost his Gallic allies by refusing to pay them at all, and impaired his country's credit by reducing the weight of his coins.

As an actual fact, all the final issues of Perseus, coined during the war with Rome, are very much lighter in weight than their predecessors. They are also of somewhat poorer style. All of Philip's tetradrachms, and fully half those of Perseus are of good Attic weight; when in fine condition they tip the scales at about seventeen grammes or more. The final issues of Perseus average only between fifteen and fifteen and a half grammes. That this reduction was of an official nature is proved by the fact that the chief magistrates' monogram on all the full weighted coins (except for the first or commemorative issue) is placed above the eagle's head, whereas on every one of the lightweight tetradrachms the monogram (in this case ΛΥ) is invariably placed in the field to the right of the eagle. Thus any one "in the know" could always distinguish the light coins without recourse to the trouble of weighing them.

Finally the Senate, wearying of the long drawn out conflict, sent a man of real character and military ability, L. Aemilius Paullus, to bring matters to a conclusion. He quickly maneuvered Perseus out of his mountain defenses into the plain of Pydna and there, on the 22nd of June, 168 B.C., inflicted upon him an absolutely disastrous defeat. The Macedonian army was practically annihilated, Perseus fled with his children to Samothrace, was captured there, and handed over to his high-minded adversary. Paullus treated him with kindness and consideration. Eventually Perseus and his two children graced the triumph of the victor — just as we see it commemorated on the denarii of Paullus'

Figure 6.

descendant. Perseus was later thrown into a dungeon, but Aemilius procured his release and he passed the remaining years of his life peacefully in the little town of Alba, near Rome. A somewhat feeble ending for a life of great promise.

The Macedonian tragedy, however, was not yet complete. After the fall of Perseus the Romans pacified the country by splitting it up into four local and mutually independent governments, in order to break the people's spirit and destroy their racial unity and material prosperity. It is therefore hardly surprising that the Macedonians, ever mindful of their glorious past, should have received with open arms a certain young adventurer from Adramyttium, one Philip Andriscus, who in 150 B.C. suddenly appeared and gave himself out as a natural son of Perseus. With the help of some Thracian chieftains he invaded eastern Macedonia and twice routed the hastily gathered local militia under Roman command. The Macedonians now rose to a man, drove out the Roman officials and proclaimed Andriscus king.

In 149 B.C. the Roman praetor, P. Iuventius Thalna, captured Amphipolis and held it long enough to strike some rare tetradrachms. But he had only one legion with him and it was not long before he and his entire force were defeated and he himself

Figure 7.

lost his life. In 148 B.C. his successor, the praetor Q. Caecilius Metellus, invaded Macedonia from the west, lost a minor engagement near Pydna, but eventually defeated Andriscus, drove him into Thrace where he again defeated him. Andriscus sought refuge with the Thracian chieftain Byzes, who however soon delivered him over to Metellus. Thus disastrously ended the abortive attempt of the Macedonians to throw off the Roman yoke.

During Andriscus' two years' rule, autonomous tetradrachms (Fig. 6) were coined in the name of the Macedonian people, as also tetradrachms (Fig. 7) in Philip's own name. The latter are copied directly from the issues of Philip V. On the obverse appears the now usual Macedonian shield with the youthful head of Andriscus in the center. As on the coins of Philip V, he wears the winged, griffin-headed helmet but, unlike Philip, he is represented without a beard. On the reverse we again see the club surrounded by an oak wreath. But while Philip V's issues are always provided with three monograms in the field and a symbol outside the wreath, Andriscus' coins bear neither monogram nor symbol, though at times a letter (M) appears outside the wreath.

EIGHT

PHILETAERUS

PERHAPS one of the most interesting characters to be found among the later followers of Alexander the Great was the eunuch Philetaerus, Lord of Pergamum.

Raised in the busy little Greco-Bithynian town of Tium, we first hear of Philetaerus being carried by his nurse to watch an important funeral — probably that of some local "big shot" or racketeer. But, unfortunately, the crowd was terrific and the poor little fellow was badly crushed in the jam and was seriously maimed. By sheer capacity, however, he rose above physical disabilities to become an officer in the army of Docimus, one of Antigonus' generals. Now in those stirring times the political scene resembled nothing so much as an ever shifting kaleidoscope — soon Antigonus lost life and empire on the fatal battlefield of Ipsus against the coalition of his bitter rivals, Cassander of Macedon, Lysimachus of Thrace, and Seleucus of Babylonia.

Tetradrachm of Lysimachus.

Philetaerus adroitly weathered the change and became a lieutenant of the crafty Lysimachus. He must indeed have made an extraordinary impression upon his new lord and master, for Lysimachus before long placed him in charge of his treasure of nine thousand talents (several millions of dollars in our money), stored for safety's sake in the strong fortress at Pergamum. And for Lysimachus — whose reputation among his contemporaries was that of a suspicious and stingy old miser — to trust Philetaerus to that extent meant that he must already have proved himself a man of outstanding steadfastness and integrity of character. As treasurer for Lysimachus he now struck many coins at Pergamum bearing the name and types of his exacting master.

Tetradrachm of Philetaerus with portrait of Seleucus.

This lovely picture, however, was not of many years' duration. Eventually court intrigues, instigated by that beautiful but scheming lady, Arsinoe, wife of Lysimachus and the future queen of Egypt, followed by the judicial murder of the heir apparent to whom Philetaerus was closely attached, placed the latter in an awkward and dangerous position. Fearing for his own safety, he now wrote to Seleucus asking for help in return for his allegiance and, above all, the treasures under his care. In 282 B.C. Seleucus with a great army crossed the Taurus Mountains, invaded Asia Minor, captured Sardes and utterly defeated the outraged Lysimachus hastening to defend his empire. Lysimachus perished in the final battle and his realms fell to Seleucus — the last of Alexander's band of heroes.

Philetaerus thus successfully shifted his allegiance and was now the subject of a new master, in return for which he remained in charge of the treasure and ruler of the little district of Pergamum together with its surrounding mountains and the fertile valley running down to the sea. Again Philetaerus had safely ridden the political breakers and was more firmly intrenched than ever.

Alas! within seven short months Seleucus was treacherously assassinated, his army went over to the murderer, his empire all but fell to pieces, Gallic hordes burst into Asia from across the Hellespont. Philetaerus on his mountain top, and with a jealously guarded treasure at his command, had little to fear. By timely and judicious outlays of cash (he ransomed the body of the murdered Seleucus for the sake of his son Antiochus; he made gifts to the towns of Pitane and Cyzicus for public works or to defend themselves against the devastating Gauls); he secured the good will of his neighbors. He threw in his wealth and power to aid Antiochus I, Seleucus' son and heir, in the latter's darkest hours — and was again rewarded by unquestioned title to Pergamum and its treasure. He now struck many coins, first in Seleucus' name, later in his own name but bearing Seleucus'

portrait. For eighteen years longer Philetaerus remained loyal to his latest suzerain, and finally died in his eightieth year (263 B.C.), honored and respected by all, and ruler of a compact and rich little province of great future promise. His sorrowing people at once deified him.

Philetaerus' nephew and successor Eumenes I thereupon instituted a large and important coinage whose types lasted more or less unchanged until the end of the dynasty in 133 B.C. On the reverse we see a beautiful figure of Athena, patron goddess of Pergamum, copied from the well-known coins of the king for whom Philetaerus had first served as treasurer. The obverse is graced by a re-

Tetradrachm of Eumenes I.

Tetradrachm of Attalus I.

markable portrait of Philetaerus himself — to which we turn with considerable interest and curiosity. The head is encircled by the taenia, symbol of divinity. In spite of the truly Greek delicacy of plane and contour the features display almost the brutal frankness of Roman portraiture. The face itself is somewhat over-full, as was only to have been expected. The fatness of cheek and jowl, however, cannot hide the firm and powerful jaw beneath, which lends the face its sense of power and resistless determination. The eye is small and perhaps crafty, but with a direct, intense, even piercing gaze. A glance suffices to remove all doubt that the features are in full accord with what we know or can surmise of the history and character of this remarkable man — the eunuch Philetaerus.

NINE

THE KINGS
OF BITHYNIA

FOUR generations of petty chieftains are known to have maintained a somewhat precarious independence in the hills of Bithynia, under Persian suzerainty. They succeeded, moreover, in completely defying the Macedonians who late in the fourth century tried to subdue them. Eventually one Zipoetes became powerful enough to assume the title of king in 297 B.C., which year commences the era used by the later kings in dating their coins.

Figure 1.

Zipoetes' son, Nicomedes I (circa 278-250 B.C.), greatly extended his power by boldly hiring and incorporating into his army the fierce Gaulish invaders of Greece and Thrace. Some ten years later he founded the flourishing seaport of Nicomedia, and here minted his well-known tetradrachms (Fig. 1) and drachms. The portrait on their obverses reveal to us the rugged features of a strong-willed, able and pertinacious man. On the reverses of his tetradrachms is seated Bendis, the Artemis of the Thracians; while the drachms show a seated figure of Ares — all done in the best Hellenistic style.

No silver coins are known of his son Ziaelas (circa 250-228 B.C.), but tetradrachms again appear in large

Figure 2.

Figure 3.

numbers under the latter's successor Prusias I (228 — circa 185 B.C.). Prusias' features are at first reproduced (Fig. 2) in a slightly idealized form, but his later issues present (Fig. 3) a very individual portrait with prominent nose and "sideburns," reminding us strongly of the "Beau Brummels" of the Regency period in England. The reverse type is always an imposing figure of Zeus, standing and crowning the king's name. There is good reason for believing that in this type we may recognize a close version of the famous statue of Zeus Stratios by the Bithynian sculptor

[44]

Doedalsos, who flourished about the middle of the third century B.C. The statue itself stood in the great temple of Zeus at Nicomedia. Prusias 1 — said to have married the sister of Philip V of Macedon — was perhaps the greatest of all the Bithynian monarchs. Among other things, he was able to subdue numerous Greek cities and add them to his realm.

Figure 4.

His son, Prusias II (185-149 B.C.), proved to be a feeble and even vicious character, described by Polybius in most unflattering terms: "King Prusias was an ill-favoured man, and though possessed of fair reasoning powers, was but half a man as regards his appearance, and had no more military capacity than a woman; for not only was he a coward, but he was incapable of putting up with hardship, and, to put it shortly, he was effeminate in body and mind through his whole life — he was entirely a stranger to literature, philosophy and all such studies, and generally speaking had no notion what-

ever of what goodness and beauty are, but lived by day and night the barbarous life of a Sardanapallus." Not surprisingly therefore do his portraits (Fig. 4) show us a heavy, stupid looking person, at first wearing a close cropped beard, later almost clean shaven. His diadem is always adorned with a wing, just above the ear. This wing probably refers to his claim, through his mother, to descent from the hero Perseus, the reputed ancestor of the royal Macedonian House of the Antigonids. In addition, Prusias II married the sister of Perseus, son of Philip V of Macedon, and thus had a double claim upon his maternal ancestor. Eventually his vicious nature led him to threaten the life of his son Nicomedes, who finally revolted and caused his despicable parent to be slain at the altar of Zeus (whose statue appears on all our coins) in Nicomedia.

Figure 5.

Nicomedes II Epiphanes (149 — circa 120 B.C.) was a man of different stamp and made repeated attempts to enlarge his kingdom. He was not so abjectly subservient to the Romans as his father had been, though he allied himself with them whenever his interests so dictated. His rather over-size, thin and spread tetradrachms (Fig. 5) continue the same reverse type of the standing Zeus as found on the coins of his father and grandfather. His own portrait, on the obverse, reveals to us a man with a strong tendency to obesity, but possessing withal an alert and determined air. Fortunately for us these tetradrachms are dated and continue in a practically unbroken series from the year of his accession (ΘMP=149 B.C.) until his death.

His successors, all bearing the now sacred name of Nicomedes, continued to coin — like the Ptolemies and the Attalids — with the same types and inscriptions as their great namesake, Nicomedes II, so that only the dates and the increasing poorness of the style allow us to distinguish their several coinages. Nicomedes III Euergetes (circa 120 — 94 B.C.) proved even more independent of Rome than his father had been, and at one time became the ally of Mithradates the Great of Pontus. Together they seized Paphlagonia and Galatia, but came to blows over Cappadocia which they both coveted. Nicomedes tricked his ally by suddenly marrying the Cappadocian Queen-Regent Laodice, thinking thus to make good his claim to that country. The wrathful Mithradates, however, soon chased his whilom ally out. The quarrel continued until finally the Romans intervened by taking Cappadocia from Mithradates, and Paphlagonia from Nicomedes.

Nicomedes IV Philopator (94-74 B.C.) was ousted in 91 B.C. by his rebellious brother Socrates, but was restored the following year by the Romans. When in 88 B.C. Mithradates suddenly swept over Asia Minor, Philopator fled from his kingdom, but was later, in 84 B.C., restored again by Sulla's legate Curio. At his death in 74 B.C. it was found that he had willed Bithynia to the Roman people. His last tetradrachm bears the date ΔKΣ (74-3 B.C.), the actual year in which Bithynia became absorbed into Roman possessions in Asia Minor.

TEN

THE KINGS
OF PONTUS

ALTHOUGH the direct ancestors of the so-called Mithradatic dynasty of Pontus had played an important role at Cius in Bithynia even before the third century B.C., it is not our intention to discuss them here. Our interest commences only after the dynasty had already become established in Pontus.

Figure 1.

The first of its sovereigns to strike portrait coins was Mithradates III (circa 246-190 B.C.) who issued some handsome but very rare tetradrachms (Fig. 1) with an extraordinarily realistic portrait on the obverse and the enthroned Zeus of the old Alexander coinage on the reverse. In the field can be seen the star and crescent, a symbol that continued to appear as a sort of family badge on all the Pontic royal coinage for many years afterwards. In this case, it doubtless represented the sun and moon, and was symbolic of the Persian royal descent claimed by a family which continued to profess the old Iranian religion.

Pharnaces I (circa 190-169 B.C.) and Mithradates IV (circa 169-150 B.C.) succeeded in their turn, and also struck splendid portrait tetradrachms — all equally difficult to ob-

Figure 2.

tain. Strange physiognomies, strongly indicative of their non-Greek origin, do these kings present on their coins. No less strange are the reverse types. Pharnaces adopts a composite male divinity (Fig. 2) wearing the petasus of Hermes and carrying in his hand the vine branch and cornucopiae of Dionysus, together with the caduceus of Hermes. He is accompanied by a deer or stag. Mithradates IV chose for his reverse type the standing figure of the hero Perseus, holding the Gorgo's head and his usual hooked sword (the harpa).

In 120 B.C. there succeeded to the Pontic throne that strange and erratic genius, Mithradates VI Eupator, who, for a time, held all Asia Minor in thrall and caused even mighty Rome to shudder at his name. For nine years the regency was exercised by the queen-mother Laodice, who during this period struck some excessively rare tetradrachms bearing her portrait. But in 111 B.C. the restless and rebellious spirit of Mithradates, now a young man of twenty, could no longer brook control; by a "coup d'état" and the assassination of his mother he seized the power. One by one, though negotiation or successful war, he added to his patrimony the provinces of Lesser Armenia, Cholcis and the Tauric Chersonese — in other words, the entire southern, eastern and northern shores of the Black Sea from Heraclea to the neighborhood of modern Odessa. There followed (about 105 B.C.) an alliance with Nicomedes of Bithynia for a joint war of conquest against Paphlagonia, Galatia and Cappadocia. These were conquered, but a dog fight over the spoils ensued between the victors until eventually Rome intervened and restored Paphlagonia and Cappadocia to their rightful owners (97 B.C.).

Mithradates never forgave Rome for what appeared to him as an unwarranted intrusion into his affairs. From that time forth he was her bitterest enemy. He at once set about preparations, sometimes secret, sometimes open, for the coming struggle. Alliances were formed; his agents placed at strategic points throughout Asia; his armies recruited and thoroughly trained and equipped; and, last but not least, a large coinage in

gold and silver inaugurated to furnish him with the "sinews of war."

A few preliminary, undated tetradrachms had already been struck, probably shortly after the young king had seized the power from his mother. On the obverse of these coins (Fig. 3) appears a youthful and spirited portrait of the king, a faint beard showing about his cheeks and jaw. On the reverse, winged Pegasus lowers his head to drink of the Pierian Spring. The usual star and crescent is in the field, and the whole design is generally surrounded by a wreath of ivy leaves and blossoms. This wreath, of course, bears an allusion to the epithet of Dionysus, which Mithradates had assumed, and was copied from the far-spread cistophoric coinage of Asia Minor. Pegasus refers to the dynastic claim of a descent from the hero Perseus.

In the two hundred and second year of the Pontic era, which is 96/5 B.C. or the year following the humiliating intervention of Rome, Mithradates took the significant step of commencing a large and steady coinage of gold and silver. These coins are not only dated by the year but also by the month, so that we are hereby enabled to check upon the annual output, down to a very close point. We can clearly see how Mithradates was marshalling his resources for his promised revenge. The coins themselves are similar to the earlier issues, except for the dates and the portrait, which is now clean shaven and more mature.

Mithradates took advantage (91 B.C.) of Rome's preoccupation with her Civil Wars to drive Nicomedes out of Bithynia. He was restored by

Figure 3.

the Romans in 89 B.C., and trusting in their continued support, himself foolishly invaded Mithradates' lands. This was the last straw and brought about the final rupture. Mithradates felt himself fully prepared, and like lightning did he strike. All Asia rose at his bidding against the hated oppressors. In one day eighty thousand Romans and Latins are said to have perished in this bloody "Sicilian Vespers" of antiquity. The Roman armies, together with those of their allies, were routed and scattered, the débris seeking refuge here and there on islands off the coast. Asia was freed. Mithradates himself chose Pergamum as his capital and royal residence. His armies invaded Macedonia and Greece, while Athens, in festive mood, received his representatives with loud acclaim. To bind her yet further to his cause, gold and silver was poured into the city, from which that once proud republic struck coins bearing not only the star and crescent emblem of Mithradates' dynasty, but even his own name and royal title.

Figure 4.

Other Asiatic cities, such as Ephesus, Erythrae, Priene, Tralles, struck gold coins of autonomous types from metal which Mithradates furnished them to assure their continued support. Mithradates himself, as befitted so great an occasion, opened a royal mint at Pergamum from whence there now flowed forth a gorgeous series of gold staters and silver tetradrachms. These (Fig. 4) bear a large, idealized but rather theatrical portrait of Mithradates, with flowing diadem ends and dramatically flying locks of hair. On the reverse, instead of the customary Pegasus, we see a feeding stag. In the field appears the monogram of Pergamum and a new set of dates, running from one to four, counted from the day on which his great crusade against Rome had triumphed. In the meanwhile, the usual coinage continued in the Pontus, with its more restrained portrait, its drinking Pegasus and its Pontic dates (years 209 to the sixth month of 212).

But Rome was not thus easily disposed of. Recovering from the first numbing shock of the disaster, the republic raised a veteran army which, under the command of the renowned Sulla, invaded Greece, besieged and captured Athens (86 B.C.), routed Mithradates' generals in the field, and drove them headlong out of Europe. Asia was next invaded, battles won, the cities induced to rise again against their recent "saviour" — and Mithradates' delirious dream was over. By the treaty of Dardanus (85/4 B.C.) he delivered up all his conquests and the greater part of his fleet, paid an enormous indemnity and retired within his former frontiers. With the evacuation of Pergamum, his issues there naturally ceased, but the idealized portrait and the feeding stag were adopted by the Pontic issues (middle of the year 212 = 85 B.C.), and continued until the end of his reign.

The ensuing ten years were ones of recuperation and defense of his own borders against aggression by irresponsible Roman generals and their allies. Finally in 74 B.C. the third Mithradatic war broke out upon the death of Nicomedes of Bithynia, who had left his kingdom to Rome in his will. Mithradates had indeed been preparing for renewed hostilities, by rebuilding his army, rearming it and training it after the Roman pattern. At first he swept all before him, the consul Cotta was utterly defeated near Chalcedon, and the important city and fortress of Cyzicus besieged. But Lucullus now arrived in Asia. Mithradates was forced to raise the siege, retreated with great loss to Pontus where a final battle was fought in which he was completely defeated. He fled to his son-in-law Tigranes in Armenia. Here the war was continued with alternate success and defeat. In 67 B.C. Mithradates carried out a successful diversion into Pontus and reconquered all his territories. In that very year, the two hundred and thirty first of the Pontic Era, was struck the last tetradrachm which we possess of Mithradates.

In 66 B.C. the great Pompey replaced Lucullus. Mithradates was finally defeated, and fled to Panticapaeum in the Bosporus. There he attempted to raise a new army, and even laid bold plans of gathering together the wild tribes of Sarmatians and Getae; of crossing the Danube and invading Italy from the north. But his subjects were heartily sick of war. His own son Pharnaces rebelled and was joined by both the army and the populace of Panticapaeum. Seeing that all was lost, Mithradates committed suicide in 63 B.C. No more fitting epitaph may be found for this extraordinary man than the words of Cicero which not only proclaim him the greatest of all kings after Alexander but also a more formidable opponent than any other monarch yet encountered by the Roman army.

ELEVEN

THE KINGS
OF CAPPADOCIA

THE line of the Cappadocian kings traces back historically to one Ariarathes, by common consent called

Figure 1.

Figure 2.

the First, who took advantage of the weakening power of Persia and the expedition of Alexander the Great to make himself Satrap of the high, central plateau of Asia Minor known as Cappadocia. His only coins, inscribed with his name in Aramaic characters, are imitations either of the issues of Sinope (Fig. 1) or of Mazaeus (Fig. 2), the Persian Satrap of Cilicia. His immediate successors, Ariarathes II and Ariaramnes, appear to have struck only rare copper coins. The latter's son, Ariarathes III, issued the first Cappadocian tetradrachm, an excessively rare coin of which only a single specimen has so far survived.

It is with Ariarathes IV, surnamed Eusebes, that the coins of the Cappadocian dynasty become common. While still of tender age, he succeeded

his father in 220 B.C. and reigned successfully until 163. At first an ally of the Syrian king Antiochus III, he

Figure 3.

married as his second wife the latter's daughter Antiochis in 192 B.C. Ariarathes maintained his power by eventually deserting his father-in-law after the battle of Magnesia (189 B.C.) and allying himself with the Romans and their protégé Eumenes II of Pergamum. He struck some scarce tetradrachms in the 29th and 30th years of his reign, that is, soon after his marriage with Antiochis and during the time the two sovereigns were preparing for the impending war with Rome. His drachms are quite common and bear numerous dates. Especially common are those of the 33rd year (Fig. 3), which fact has been accounted for by the statements of Livy and Polybius that in this very year (188 B.C.) the Romans forced Ariarathes to pay a huge indemnity for the aid given by him to Antiochus III. The coinage of Ariarathes IV established the customary types for all later Cappadocian coins: *obverse*, Diademed head of the king; *reverse*, Athena Nicephoros standing with spear and shield in her left hand. The king's features seem to have been handsome, but with a growing tendency towards fullness as the years go on.

His son Ariarathes V (163-130 B.C.), surnamed Eusebes Philopator, also struck numerous tetradrachms (Fig. 4) and drachms in the first three

years of his reign. His features bear a distinct resemblance to those of his father, though somewhat less full and with a more prominent nose. Ariarathes V was probably the greatest of the Cappadocian kings. He Helenized the country and intervened successfully in the affairs of Armenia, Commagene, Syria and Pergamum. During his reign rose the usurper Orophernes who attained to an ephemeral power by the aid of the Syrian king Demetrius I. To the numismatist Orophernes is especially known by the existence of some tetradrachms, as handsome as they are rare, which were found many years ago imbedded in the pedestal which Orophernes had dedicated to Athena at Priene.

Figure 5.

The youngest son of Ariarathes V, known as Ariarathes VI Epiphanes (130 — circa 112 B.C.), succeeded to

the throne after his five elder brothers had all been done away with by their ambitious and unscrupulous mother in an effort to maintain her own regency. No tetradrachms are known, only drachms (Fig. 5) bearing regnal dates from one to fifteen. The features of this prince resemble those of his grandfather.

Figure 6.

Ariarathes VI was assassinated about 112 B.C. by a certain nobleman named Gordius, and the former's eldest son Ariarathes VII, surnamed Philometor, reigned in his stead. Again, only drachms (Fig. 6) are known, bearing regnal dates from six to twelve. His was an agitated and tragic reign. His mother was Laodice, sister of Mithradates the Great of Pontus, who ruled the kingdom as regent for the young boy. Nicomedes of Bithynia later married Laodice and seized the land. Mithradates intervened on behalf of his nephew, chased out the Bithynians and restored Ariarathes VII to his throne. Eventually, however, the two disagreed and Mithradates invaded Cappadocia. In the presence of the two armies he assassinated Ariarathes and established his own son as Cappadocian king. The coins of Philometor show an attractive, youthful face with a finely arched nose.

The Cappadocians, however, did not acquiesce so readily in this new state of affairs and rebelled against the usurper. They recalled from exile another son of Ariarathes VI, but Mithradates soon disposed of him and no coins of his (Ariarathes VIII) are known to exist. In the meanwhile Mithradates' son also assumed the name Ariarathes (now the ninth, with the titles of Eusebes Philopator) and proceeded to rule over the Cappadocians. He struck drachms (Fig. 7),

Figure 7.

of the usual Cappadocian type, with his portrait on the obverse which bears a striking resemblence to his father, Mithradates the Great. He also issued some handsome, but rare, tetradrachms (Fig. 8) closely modeled

Figure 8.

on his father's Pontic coinage. On the obverse we see a very realistic portrait of Ariarathes IX, while the reverse type is the feeding Pegasus surrounded by a vine wreath. These tetradrachms are supposed to have been minted at Amphipolis in Macedonia when in 87 B.C. Ariarathes was in titular command of his father's

army in those regions. His drachms, however, were certainly struck in Cappadocia.

Figure 9.

Figure 10.

With the year 96 B.C. a new dynasty made its appearance. One Ariobarzanes, of the Cappadocian nobility, was chosen to be king. His assumed title, Philoromaios, attests both his policy and his real supporters. He struck only drachms (Figs. 9 and 10), with the usual Cappadocian reverse type of the standing Athena, accompanied by regnal dates running intermittently from two to thirty-four. This very much broken series of dates reflects clearly the peculiarly vicissitudinous character of his reign. In 93 B.C. he was driven out by Tigranes of Armenia, replaced by Sulla in 92, chased out by Mithradates in 91, replaced by L. Cassius and Q. Oppius in 90, again chased out by Mithradates in 89, replaced by Curio in 84, driven out, once more, in 81, only to be immediately replaced the same year by Murena, driven out by Tigranes in 77 and by Mithradates in 74, replaced by Lucullus in 73, once more driven out by the combined forces of Mithradates and Tigranes in 67, replaced by Pompey in 66 — and finally forced by the latter in 63 B.C. to abdicate in favor of his son. With such a career it is a living wonder that Ariobarzanes I ever found time to strike any coins at all! His mint must surely have been mounted on wheels! Interesting it is to follow through the years the development of his portrait from a smooth faced young man (Fig. 9) with a prominent nose of "Roman" type, to that of an old man (Fig. 10) with sunken cheeks, heavily wrinkled brow and hawk-like nose.

Valerius Maximus gives us a touching description of the final scene: "Ariobarzanes abdicated his throne in the presence of Cn. Pompey. He was present at an audience with that general, and at his invitation mounted the tribunal and seated himself upon a curule chair. But perceiving his own son near the balustrade, in a corner of the tribunal — place unworthy of his rank — he could not bear to see him thus standing below himself. At once he descended, placed the diadem upon his brow, and urged him to occupy the seat which he had just left. The eyes of the young prince filled with tears, he trembled all over, he let fall the diadem and had not the strength to take one step towards the place pointed out to him. What an almost incredible sight, to behold with what joy the one deposed the diadem and with what sadness the other received it! This generous strife might have had no end, had not the authority of Pompey intervened in favor of the paternal wish. He gave to the son the title of king, had him accept the diadem and forced him to seat himself upon the curule chair." To us, in view of the elder man's experiences, the joy to relinquish and the reluctance

to accept the diadem hardly seem so strange! The whole scene was probably all "arranged" beforehand — but it makes a good story none the less.

Ariobarzanes II Philopator (63—52 B.C.) now reigned in his father's place and struck the usual drachms which bear the regnal dates seven

Figure 11.

(Fig. 11) and eight. According to his portrait, he had apparently inherited his father's masterful nose, but his face is thinner and of a bonier structure.

In 52 B.C. he was succeeded by his son, Ariobarzanes III Eusebes Philoromaios, who reigned until 42 B.C.

Figure 12.

and struck drachms (Fig. 12) dated in his ninth and eleventh years. His is the first Cappadocian portrait with a beard. For the first time, also, there appears in the field of the reverse a star and crescent symbol — emblem of the Pontic kings. This fact has given Reinach a sure basis for his brilliant conjecture that the little daughter of Mithradates the Great, known to have been espoused to an Ariobarzanes, must actually have married Ariobarzanes II and so become the mother of Ariobarzanes III. Cicero has occasion to speak of this lady's haughtiness and ability for devious intrigue — well-known characteristics of the Pontic kings, her royal ancestors.

Figure 13.

In 42 B.C. Ariobarzanes was executed by order of Cassius, and soon after, Marc Antony filled the vacant Cappadocian throne in the person of Ariobarzanes' brother, Ariarathes X Eusebes Philadelphus. The last ruler of that name now proceeded to strike the usual drachms (Fig. 13) in the fifth and sixth years of his reign. His is indeed a strange and not very pleasing physiognomy, with his enormous nose, under-shot jaw, bearded lip and chin.

In 36 B.C. Ariarathes X and Marc Antony fell out. Antony had him executed and replaced by one Archelaus, great grandson of Mithradates' famous general of the same name, grandson and son of two generations of high priests of the ancient and far renowned sanctuary of the Mother Goddess at Comana. Although faithful to Antony during the civil wars

Archelaus was, none the less, continued in his rule by the victorious Augustus who gave him, in addition, Little Armenia and Cilicia Trachea.

Figure 14.

Figure 15.

He eventually died in Rome, 17 A.D., at an advanced age. He struck dated drachms and hemi-drachms; the former (Fig. 14) of fine style with his portrait on the obverse and the club of Heracles on the reverse; the latter (Fig. 15) with a head of Heracles on the obverse and an interesting representation of the sacred Mount Argaeus on the reverse.

Thus comes to an end the long line of Cappadocian drachms, bearing the life-like portraits of three dynasties of kings who in their day had played a leading role in the affairs of Asia Minor.

TWELVE

THE ARMENIAN KINGS

THE early history of Armenia, like that of many another Asiatic state, is lost in obscurity, which in this case has been made yet denser by the foolish fables and pseudo-histories of Armenian chroniclers. Under the Achaemenid kings this mountainous and difficult country was included in the thirteenth satrapy — but actually it enjoyed practical independence. The Seleucid kings managed to dominate it at various times, but after the battle of Magnesia (189 B.C.) Armenia again became independent. The country was divided into two portions, Greater and Lesser Armenia, each ruled by its own princes. Many of their names we know from scattered historical notices or from their rare copper coins which, from time to time, come to light. Charaspes, Arsames, Abdissares and Xerxes have all left numismatic records. But unfortunately these coins, so interesting because of the portraits they bear, are every one extremely rare.

With the advent to power of Tigranes I, surnamed the Great (97-56 B.C., or, according to others, 94-54 B.C.), a new and glorious era dawns for the Armenian state. Tigranes had been brought up as a hostage at the court of the great Mithradates II, king of Parthia. He must there have won that monarch's esteem and friendship, for it was through his favor that Tigranes secured the throne. The young man immediately set about widening his ancestral domains, adding Sophene, and later, during the troubles which befell Parthia on the death of Mithradates II (circa 91 B.C.), reconquering all the districts which the Armenian had ceded to his powerful neighbor in exchange for the latter's support. Lesser Armenia was next secured, and Tigranes found himself ruler over a united and powerful state. Not content with this, he formed an alliance with Mithradates VI of Pontus, whose daughter he married; he intervened in the affairs of Cappadocia; he seized the provinces of Gordyene (northern Kurdistan,) Atropatene (Azerbeijan), Adiabene (district about Mosul), Nisibis and Osrhoene (Edessa) in Mesopotamia.

He assumed the proud oriental title of "King of Kings" — a title which until his recent death had been borne by Tigranes' patron, Mithradates II of Parthia. Tigranes' good fortune must now have seemed invincible, and he reached out to make good the greatest ambition of his life, namely the acquisition of what remained of the once mighty Seleucid empire. That unhappy and shrunken state was at this time divided into two portions. The feeble Philip ruled over Cilicia and Syria proper, with his capital at Antioch. His brother Antiochus XII had from Damascus ruled the province of Coele-Syria until 84 B.C. when he fell in battle against the Arabs. The Damascus garrison had then called in Aretas, king of the Nabataeans.

About the year 83 B.C. the Syrians, disgusted with the ineptitude of their legitimate prince and somewhat dazzled by the splendor of Tigranes' achievements, called upon the latter to rule over them. With alacrity the Armenian king responded and with little apparent difficulty secured the greater part of Philip's domains. The latter completely disappears from history and his actual fate is unknown. Proud of his astounding success — as well he might be — Tigranes decided to found a new capital worthy of his fame and empire. In northern Mesopotamia, between Edessa and Nisibis, there arose circa 77 B.C. the walls and towers of Tigranocerta, more centrally located than the teeming but unstable Syrian metropolis of Antioch, or even of his own mountain capital of Artaxata near Erivan, in the shadow of Mount Ararat. Tigranes had now reached the apogee of his power.

Figure 1.

Instead of the modest copper coinage of his Armenian predecessors, a more ambitious and opulent series of silver tetradrachms is now introduced by Tigranes to replace the issues of the former Seleucid empire. The principal mint was of course located in the great and populous city of Antioch, through whose market places flowed the wealth and commerce of Asia. On the obverses of the new coinage (Fig. 1) we may behold a striking portrait of Tigranes himself, clean shaven according to Greek taste, but wearing a towering Armenian tiara with broad flaps, its upper portion richly embroidered with star and eagles, topped with numerous points or zig-zags (to symbolize the rays of the sun?) and bordered throughout with pearls. A broad diadem also encircles his head, is knotted at the back, the ends falling in a graceful curve behind. The reverse type is, if anything, still more interesting. A female figure, draped in a mantle and wearing a mural crown upon her head, is seated to the right upon a rock. In her hand she grasps a palm branch, while beneath her foot a youthful male figure is depicted in the act of swimming. Obviously we have before us the earliest numismatic representation of the famous statue of the Tyche of Antioch, seated upon Mt. Sipylus, the personification of the Orontes swimming in the river at her feet. This gilded bronze statue, renowned throughout all antiquity, was the work of the great sculptor Eutychides of Sicyon, a pupil of Lysippus. Seleucus I is said to have erected the statue near the banks of the Orontes, placing it in shrine, open on all sides and supported by four columns — exactly as we find it reproduced on later bronze coins of the Roman emperors from Trajan Decius to Valerian.

Figure 2.

When Tigranes had added Damascus to his realm, he struck there a further series of tetradrachms (Fig. 2).

But instead of the seated Antioch, these coins bear a figure of the Tyche of Damascus, similarly seated on a rock with the river Chrysaroas at her feet. In this case, however, the goddess is turned to the left, her right arm is stretched out before her, her left supports a cornucopiae. Fortunately, these coins all bear dates according to the Seleucid Era (AMΣ = 72/1 B.C.; BMΣ = 71/0 B.C.; ΓMΣ = 70/69 B.C.) so that we are thereby informed of the years in which Tigranes ruled over Damascus — a fact not mentioned by a single ancient historian. Significantly enough, this coinage comes to an end the very year in which the jerry-built empire of Tigranes commenced to tumble about his ears.

The great Lucullus, commander-in-chief of the Roman armies in Asia, had finally defeated Mithradates, who fled to Armenia for refuge. In 69 B.C. the Roman general decided to call Tigranes to account for his past misdeeds and hostility to the Eternal City. With a small but veteran army Lucullus crossed the Euphrates, marched through Sophene and laid siege to Tigranocerta. At the same time he completely routed, in the open field, an immense army which Tigranes had led to the relief of his capital. All of Tigranes' Syrian possessions now fell away, as one of the last scions of the Seleucid race, Antiochus XIII, arrived at Antioch and was received with open arms by the fickle populace. Troubles came thick and fast upon the king. One of his sons rebelled, two others were executed on suspicion, Tigranocerta fell, Lucullus invaded (68 B.C.) Armenia itself and laid siege to Artaxata. The

city was only saved by mutiny in the Roman army, and Lucullus was called off by a sudden disaster which befell his lieutenant Triarius in Pontus. In 66 B.C. Pompey arrived in Asia and replaced Lucullus.

Figure 3.

Having disposed of Mithradates, Pompey proceeded (64 B.C.) to Syria in order to settle the affairs of the East. Syria was made a Roman province inclusive of all the land this side of the Euphrates. Tigranes had suffered enough, and made haste to offer himself in abject submission to Pompey. He was deprived of all his conquered provinces, but northern Mesopotamia was returned to him and he was allowed to continue as king of Armenia under a sort of Roman protectorate. After things had settled down a bit, Tigranes commenced to issue his third series of silver coins. These, probably struck at Tigranocerta, comprise drachms (Fig. 3) and rare tetradrachms with types very similar to the former issues of the Antioch mint. Not only do these new coins now bear, for the first time, Tigranes' full title of "King of Kings," but they are also dated with his regnal years 35, 36, 37 and 38—showing that they were coined towards the very end of his reign.

On the death of Tigranes his surviving son Artavasdes (56—30 B.C.?) came to the throne. Other rulers eventually followed, of whom may be mentioned Tigranes II (circa 20 — 12

B.C.), Tigranes III (12 — 6 B.C.), and Artavasdes III (2 — 10 A.D.). Gradually Armenia had become re-

Figure 4.

duced to its original mountain cantons, for it led a somewhat tortured existence as a buffer state between the powerful and hostile empires of Rome and Parthia. Whatever the varying outcome of the wars waged between these protagonists of East and West, it was invariably Armenia that had the most to suffer. Small wonder therefore that her numismatic output dwindled more and more, until it finally vanished completely, its place being taken by the imported coins of her two neighbors. Of the later Armenian kings, mentioned above, only a few exceedingly rare drachms (Fig. 4, a coin of Tigranes II) and accompanying bronze coins have survived. These are most interesting, not only on account of their great rarity but also because they continue to furnish us with lifelike portraits of these kings (so often mentioned by Roman historians) who strove so valiantly to preserve their country intact between the upper and nether millstones of Rome and Parthia.

THIRTEEN

THE SUCCESSORS
OF SELEUCUS

WHEN in 280 B.C. old Seleucus fell by the assassin's dagger, his son Antiochus was ruling as viceroy in distant Babylonia. With the heir so far away, the wide-spread and laboriously erected empire threatened to disintegrate. Cities and provinces commenced to act independently, subject princes to rebel, neighboring kings to seize outlying districts. The fierce Gauls also burst into Asia Minor, burning and plundering wherever they went, spreading terror and destruction throughout the richest provinces.

While not quite the equal of his father in ability, Antiochus I nevertheless faced these many dangers with fortitude. By dint of constant marching from danger point to danger point, by many hard fought campaigns and perpetual vigilance, he eventually managed to maintain his heritage substantially intact.

fine tetradrachms (Fig. 1) bearing a splendid head of his deified sire, adorned with diadem and bull's horn — symbols of royalty and power. The reverses of these coins have a seated Apollo, probably the first appearance of a type which was destined to remain for many generations the favorite device of the Seleucid kings. Here Apollo, seated upon an omphalos and holding a bow, is honored as the reputed divine ancestor of the dynasty. Later Antiochus placed his own portrait upon his coinage, Apollo remaining his constant companion on the reverse. Early in his reign we see

Figure 2.

Figure 1.

Figure 3.

Throughout his reign Antiochus struck many coins. At first he continued his father's issues of the old Alexander type, but now in his own name. At one of the western mints, for a brief space, he brought out some

Antiochus (Fig. 2) as a man of middle age, with strong nose, sunken eye, and somewhat beetling brow. But his exhausting attempts to maintain his empire and ward off his envious rivals eventually left their mark, and his final portraits (Fig. 3) emphasize the sunken eye, the heavy lines on brow and cheek. Perhaps the most striking characteristic of his physiognomy is the long upper lip — a typical Hibernian "flannel-lip" — which irresistibly reminds us of some old Irishman of popular fancy.

Antiochus I died at Sardes in 261 B.C., leaving the empire which he had struggled so long to maintain, to his son Antiochus II, surnamed Theos. Of this prince we actually know very little, for the histories covering his time have largely perished. Malicious gossip at second hand from the untrustworthy Phylarchus, paints him as a confirmed drunkard, incapable and apathetic. Other historical fragments suggest a certain lack of tenacity and purpose in his character. But active he was, though not particularly successful, in numerous campaigns in Thrace, Asia Minor and against Egypt in Syria. While embroiled in these western wars, his eastern provinces fell away. In 250 B.C. Diodotus rebelled in Bactria and with hardly a struggle secured for himself this fabulously rich and populous country. Encouraged by this event the little Parthian prince Arsaces, two years later, raised the standard of revolt in the district of Astauene; thus another province was lost to the Seleucid.

Dismayed at these disasters and harassed by his western troubles, Antiochus finally made peace with Ptolemy, whose daughter Berenice he married to seal the pact. By this act were ignominiously ousted from their rightful heritage Antiochus' sister and former wife Laodice, together with

their children. Antiochus himself died (by the hand of the outraged Laodice, it is rumored) in 246 B.C.

Figure 4.

Until recently the features of Antiochus II have been as uncertain as his history — his real coins being erroneously assigned to his son Hierax, or to his grandson Antiochus III. Dr. Macdonald was the first successfully to segregate his issues, — and we now see before us (Fig. 4) a youngish man whose features do indeed bear a strong resemblance to those of his grandson. But the nose of the Second Antiochus is more rounded at the tip and not so long, his cheeks are a little more hollow and his jaw more square. He at first continued the coinage of his father unchanged, but later substituted his own portrait for that of old Antiochus. On most of his tetradrachms he retained the seated Apollo, though some scarce issues of Cyme, Myrina and Phocaea replace the sun god with a splendid seated Heracles, resting from his labors.

Having disposed of her faithless husband, Laodice proceeded to settle scores with Egyptian Berenice. A revolt was engineered at Antioch where Berenice resided, and after numerous bloody and exciting episodes that unfortunate lady was murdered just as her brother, Ptolemy III Euergetes, was leading a fleet and army to her rescue. But he took ample revenge. All Cilicia was seized, Seleucia and

Antioch captured, Syria and Mesopotamia invaded and Seleucid treasures confiscated. Eventually the victorious army returned to Egypt, laden with booty. In the meanwhile, Antiochus II's eldest son, Seleucus II, was desperately trying to raise an army in Asia Minor. When he eventually succeeded in doing so, he crossed the Taurus Mountains and chased the Egyptian garrisons, left behind by Euergetes, out of Syria and Mesopotamia. But a bad defeat at this juncture prevented him from pushing his success further, and the important seaport of Seleucia had still to be left in Egyptian hands.

Hardly had a peace been arranged with Ptolemy, when the unfortunate Seleucus learned that his brother, Antiochus, nicknamed Hierax, left behind to govern Sardes, had rebelled and claimed all Asia Minor for his own. A fratricidal war now took place between them. After a series of varying fortunes, Seleucus was finally defeated at the battle of Ancyra. It is related that when the rumor spread that Seleucus had perished in the melée, Hierax promptly went into the deepest mourning. But learning later that his dear brother was safely back in Antioch he commanded all the cities under his jurisdiction to celebrate his happy escape! Peace was now patched up between the two brothers, leaving Hierax to rule in Asia Minor, Seleucus in Syria and the east.

Accordingly, we find that the majority of Seleucus' issues were produced in the eastern half of the empire. In a few cases he retained the seated Apollo of his predecessors, but generally substituted therefor the standing figure of the god, leaning against his tripod and looking at an arrow which he holds in his extended

Figure 5.

right. The obverses of all these coins (Fig. 5) are graced by an attractive portrait of a somewhat amiable young man, handsome but for a slightly protruding upper lip and a nose that is rather too long and pointed.

Figure 6.

With regard to the coinages of the brother, perhaps the less said the better. Every scholar who has tried to handle this difficult subject has selected a different portrait and confidently claimed it to be that of Hierax. This is no place to reopen the matter. All that can safely be said is that most of the Seleucid tetradrachms which display a youthful head, whose diadem is adorned with a bird's wing (Fig. 6), were probably struck at Alexandria in the Troad during Hierax's reign. Some of these may, or may not, be his actual portrait.

Seleucus II left two sons, the elder

of whom was also named Seleucus and reigned but a short time (226-223 B.C.), being assassinated during an expedition against Attalus of Perga-

Figure 7.

mum. His coins, while not actually very rare, are known for only two or three mints, notably Antioch (Fig. 7). In features Seleucus III resembles his grandfather, rather than either his father or brother. He usually wears short side-whiskers, probably as a sign of mourning for his father.

On his death his far more famous brother, Antiochus III, ascended the Syrian throne. His was indeed a dynamic and ambitious nature. A considerable amount of ability, too, he possessed — though he probably does not really merit the title of "great," bestowed by admiring contemporaries while good fortune still smiled upon his arms. Posterity, however, has agreed to accept the title, although Antiochus' successes were more spectacular than real and were outlasted by his final disastrous failure.

Coming to the throne at the age of nineteen, Antiochus at once set about to meet the many problems confronting him. His cousin Achaeus successfully continued the war in Asia Minor, while Antiochus himself prepared to wrench Coele-Syria and Palestine from the Egyptians. But a serious revolt broke out in Media, led by its

satrap, Molon. Several royal armies were worsted and Molon eventually captured the eastern capital and all Babylonia. Here he proclaimed himself king and struck some rare copper coins. Antiochus now arrived with the main army and utterly defeated Molon, who then committed suicide.

In the meanwhile news came that Achaeus had also revolted in Asia Minor, proclaimed himself king and had made common cause with Egypt. Achaeus, too, now issued coins, in all metals. The copper are still fairly common, while the gold and silver, bearing a striking, bearded portrait of the rebel, are extremely rare.

Antiochus hastened back to Syria, captured Seleucia on the Orontes by a sudden attack, but was severely defeated by the Egyptians in the ensuing battle of Raphia. He returned north, invaded Asia Minor and, after two years of continual fighting, finally overcame Achaeus, crucified him and recovered most of the Seleucid possessions in Asia Minor.

Antiochus, now well launched in his career, decided to recover also the eastern provinces lost under his grandfather, Antiochus Theos. He attacked the Parthians and drove them back. He next moved against Euthydemus of Bactria, in whom he found a worthy opponent. After much fighting and various vicissitudes of fortune the two antagonists came to terms. Antiochus then proceeded towards India, crossed the Hindu-Kush, made a somewhat flamboyant tour through what is now modern Afghanistan and eastern Persia, received the submission of the local princes and kinglets, gathered in many elephants and much tribute, finally returning to Babylonia laden with spoils and covered with glory and renown. The world hailed him as the Great Antiochus and a new Alexander.

Thus flushed with success, Antiochus decided that the time had come for a final reckoning with Egypt, especially as, in the meanwhile, Ptolemy IV had died leaving his kingdom to an infant son, Ptolemy V Epiphanes. Antiochus, having come to a secret understanding with Philip V of Macedon for the partition of the Egyptian possessions, advanced into Coele-Syria and within two years had secured the entire country, right down to the borders of Egypt itself (198 B.C.). He next prepared to recover in Asia Minor and Thrace what still remained unredeemed of Seleucus I's conquests, even though this step would surely bring him into conflict with Rome.

At the head of his armies Antiochus swept through Asia Minor, seizing cities and provinces which had once been Seleucid. That district was at once in an uproar. Rhodes and Eumenes of Pergamum and many of the captured cities appealed loudly to Rome. Antiochus crossed the Hellespont, seized Aenus and Maronea, and commenced to rebuild Lysimachia, recently destroyed by the Thracians.

Rome now prepared for war, but in the meantime sent ambassadors and delegates armed with threats and warnings. All to no avail, for the king had by now lost all sense of proportion and utterly misjudged his own resources and ability. Encouraged by an appeal from the Aetolians, Antiochus now invaded Greece itself. He arrived there with fanfare but with an inadequate army. He was received with acclaim by the Aetolians, but lukewarmly by the remainder of the Greeks who had good cause to know the real might of Rome. Antiochus moved about as in a dream, campaigned casually in central Greece, spent the winter amid banquets and festivities at Chalcis, married a beautiful young girl, daughter of a wealthy citizen of that city, and acted generally as if Rome were non-existent.

By the spring Rome was ready. Her army landed at Apollonia and advanced into Thessaly (191 B.C.). The lukewarm Greeks fell away, the Aetolians were too weak, Antiochus' small army was routed at Thermopylae, and the king himself eventually abandoned Greece.

The following year the Romans invaded Asia Minor, and under the Consul Scipio utterly routed Antiochus and his great army at the battle of Magnesia (December 190 B.C.). Antiochus was forced to cede all Asia Minor beyond the Taurus, pay the huge indemnity of over fifteen thousand talents (roughly eighteen million gold dollars) and deliver over to Rome his own son and many other notables as hostages. As a result, most of his outlying provinces now rebelled and his kingdom was restricted to Syria, Mesopotamia and Media. He himself perished in 187/6 B.C. in an abortive attempt to plunder the rich temple of Bel and Anaitis in Susiana. He left an exhausted, impoverished and greatly depleted kingdom to his son Seleucus. The great empire which he had rebuilt with such energy and éclat proved, like Antiochus himself, to be little else than a sham, and collapsed at the devastating touch of Rome.

As might be expected, the coinages of Antiochus III are the most extensive of any of the Seleucid kings. Huge quantities of tetradrachms were coined in the leading cities of the empire.

Figure 8.

We learn of over four thousand talents, or roughly five million dollars, being turned into money at Ecbatana alone. It is typical of the man that he (the first of his line to do so) should strike great, ostentatious, octodrachms in gold. The types of both gold and silver are almost invariably the seated Apollo. On his return from the eastern campaigns he issued some interesting staters, tetradrachms (Fig. 8) and drachms bearing a stately Indian elephant on the reverse. Because of his long reign and wide dominions, the variations in his portrait are numerous, extending all the way from a youth in his teens, full of energy and the zest of life, to the disillusioned old man of his final issues. In features Antiochus III was evidently good looking, though his countenance later appears rather too bony in structure, while his pointed, aggressive nose is ill supported by a somewhat weak mouth and chin. In these is evidenced the lack of stability surprising in a man who had made such a brilliant start.

Seleucus IV faced with courage and ability the unenviable task of meeting the yearly instalments of the war in-

demnity which weighed heavily upon an exhausted and humiliated kingdom. It is the old story, which we face today, of having to pay with grinding taxes, heavy labor and unremitting thrift the glamorous reign of a brilliant, popular but unthinking

Figure 9.

and spendthrift leader. His coins (Fig. 9) depict Seleucus as a mature man, inclined to baldness, with a high forehead, large, curved nose, a determined air about his mouth and a steady look in his eye — the countenance of a man who has both feet upon the ground and is prepared to carry through a difficult, inglorious but none the less necessary task to a successful conclusion.

In the meanwhile, Seleucus' eldest son Demetrius had been sent to Rome to replace there, as hostage, Seleucus' brother Antiochus. The latter commenced a leisurely return to Syria via Athens, in which pleasant centre of art and learning he sojourned for some time. Here Antiochus made many friends, commenced the restoration of the Olympeion (the great temple of Olympian Zeus, left unfinished since the days of Peisistratus), spent money lavishly, and generally comported himself to the intense satisfaction of the good citizens of Athens who enthusiastically elected him to an important magistracy and struck coins bearing his name, accompanied by the

Seleucid elephant (Fig. 10). Suddenly news reached him that Seleucus had been assassinated and all was turmoil once more.

Figure 10.

Figure 11.

Antiochus hastened over to Asia Minor, secured the active assistance of Eumenes of Pergamum and Ariarathes of Cappadocia, with whose aid he seated himself upon the Syrian throne as Antiochus IV Epiphanes. Apparently, however, he feared the opposition of a "legitimist" party which disliked the line of succession passing directly to the brother, rather than to the son of their former king. In consequence, coins were struck bearing the usual reverse type of the seated Apollo and the inscription

Figure 12.

ΒΑΣΙΛΕΩΣ ΑΝΤΙΟΧΟΥ. Some (Fig. 11, have on their obverse Antiochus'

own features, others (Fig. 12) the baby face of a child who can only be the younger son of Seleucus, whose existence is vaguely hinted at by certain historians.

With a man of Antiochus' temperament such a state of affairs could not last long. The baby's head suddenly

Figure 13.

vanishes, and a new series of coins is brought out with a splendid, but somewhat idealized portrait of Antiochus IV on the obverse, and on the reverse a representation of his favorite divinity, Olympian Zeus (compare Fig. 13). The accompanying inscription now reads ΒΑΣΙΛΣΩΕ ΑΝΤΙΟΧΟΥ ΘΕΟΥ ΕΠΙΦΑΝΟΥΣ.

When in 171 B.C. Rome became involved in a war with Perseus of Macedon, Antiochus embraced this welcome opportunity to invade Egypt. With comparative ease he captured the old capital of Memphis and laid siege to Alexandria. Soon, however, he came to terms with the legitimate king Ptolemy VI Philometor, who accepted as co-regent Antiochus' pro= tégé Euergetes. Antiochus returned to Syria, but in 168 B.C. once more invaded Egypt as affairs had not turned out to his liking. For the two brothers had settled their quarrel and were amicably working against Seleucid interests.

Antiochus arrived before Alexandria, and was about to assault the city, when Rome's delegate, C. Popillius Laena, met him bearing an ultimatum to evacuate Egypt at once. Antiochus advanced with outstretched hands to greet his old friend from the days of his sojourn in Rome. But the Roman brusquely waved aside the proffered hand, and with his staff drew a circle in the sand around the king, demanding an answer before he should step across the line. Antiochus could do nothing else but acquiesce, with as good a grace as possible. Thereupon the two friends greeted each other warmly — but Antiochus had to lead his army ignominiously back to Syria.

In Syria once more, Antiochus appears to have vented his chagrin upon the Jews by adopting a policy of breaking the power of their priesthood, despoiling their Temple, and substituting therein the worship of Zeus for that of Jehovah. The immediate result was widespread disorder, violence and bloodshed, culminating in a desperate, and eventually successful rebellion under the inspired leadership of the Maccabees. What to Antiochus may have appeared but a minor matter, to us looms large because our knowledge of his reign is based so largely upon sources which are both directly and indirectly Jewish — and the Jewish people have never been exactly inarticulate. Hence Antiochus Epiphanes is remembered today more for his persecution of the Jews than for anything else that he may have accomplished.

Antiochus further relieved his injured feelings in a way that was, doubtless, more congenial to his basically theatrical and shallow nature. Upon hearing that the Romans were

planning to celebrate their victory over Perseus by giving at Amphipolis a splendid series of games — to which they were inviting the Hellenic world — Antiochus at once decided to put their "show" completely in the shade by giving one of his own that was to surpass anything of a similar nature that had ever before been done. Accordingly, in 166 B.C., he invited the cities and kings of Europe and Asia to attend a great religious festival to be held in the beautiful and sacred grove at Daphne, just outside Antioch. We hear of a marvelous triumphal procession, comprising fifty thousand participants, with elephants, chariots, infantry, cavalry — in purple and gold with glittering armor — long lines of young men and athletes bearing golden crowns, slaves with sacred vessels, floats with statues of the gods and with figures portraying mythical scenes or cosmic forces, bevies of beautiful girls scattering precious perfumes from golden vases. For thirty days athletic games and gladiatorial combats kept the crowds in breathless suspense, while, nightly, luxurious banquets were served to thousands of guests at a time.

Even the interest of future numismatists seems not to have been overlooked. A special series of attractive coins was issued. Among these are especially to be mentioned handsome tetradrachms whose obverses bear the heads of Antiochus' two most favored gods, Zeus or Apollo, whose features are made to resemble those of Epiphanes himself, while their reverses exhibit corresponding statues of these divinities — famous statues which could be seen and admired by the visiting crowds in the great temple of

Apollo at Daphne. We see Olympian Zeus (Fig. 14), enthroned with victory and sceptre, a copy of the world-

Figure 14.

Figure 15.

renowned masterpiece of Pheidias at Olympia which Antiochus had recently erected at Daphne. We see the Apollo Citharoedus by Bryaxis, (Fig. 15), in long robe, advancing to the sound of the lyre which he is playing. Accompanying these were also prolific issues of bronze coins, larger in size than any heretofore issued by Seleucid kings. In size and types they consciously imitate Egyptian coins, with their eagle reverses and their obverses displaying heads of Ammon and of Isis — obviously all especially designed to commemorate Antiochus' recent "triumphs" over the land of the Nile. Alongside of these, and to the end of the reign, were coined the usual tetradrachms (Fig. 13), but now

with the epithet of Nicephorus added to an already fulsome array of titles.

To the numismatist Antiochus Epiphanes thus goes out in a blaze of glory; actually, he died somewhat mysteriously on an expedition into Persia in 164 B.C. Jewish writers, followed by their Christian imitators, have woven about his demise a tissue of contradictory stories adorned with gruesome details — clearly the just vengeance of an outraged Jehovah to

Figure 16.

punish the despoiler of his Temple and the persecutor of his people!

The short and troubled reign of his nine year old son, Antiochus V Eupator, has left a few tetradrachms, with a boyish face on the obverse and the seated Zeus on the reverse (Fig. 16).

In the meanwhile, it will be remembered, Seleucus IV's oldest son Demetrius had been vegetating as a hostage at Rome. Now grown to be a personable young man of twenty-three or four, active, energetic, able, Demetrius knew that his opportunity had at last arrived. When repeated supplications to the Senate proved of no avail to release him, he took matters into his own hands. The historian Polybius was then residing in Rome and had become his fast friend. He tells us the whole story, which reads like an exciting tale of intrigue and adventure. With the connivance of certain influential Romans and the help of his many friends, a Carthaginian ship was chartered and held in readiness at Ostia. Demetrius now ostentatiously planned and departed for a great boar hunt to be held at Circei, (about where Italian kings — and Mussolini himself—were wont to hunt the boar!) and then, by night, hastened on board the waiting vessel. Thanks to well laid plans Demetrius found himself far out to sea long before even the rumor of his escape had had time to spread in Rome.

Demetrius landed safely at Tripolis in Phoenicia, and was received with open arms by the Syrians (162 B.C.). In the meanwhile, Timarchus, satrap of Media, had raised the standard of revolt, proclaimed himself king, and proceeded to strike a series of coins as befitting the occasion. While Demetrius' lieutenants were forcibly pacifying the rebellious Jews, the rightful king advanced eastwards to recover his lost provinces. Demetrius was entirely successful and signalized his victory by calling in Timarchus' issues and overstriking them with his own types — hence no doubt, the great rarity today of the usurper's coins.

Demetrius proved himself a better soldier than he did a statesman. While he consolidated his territories and maintained peace therein, he managed to arouse the fear and active hostility of his neighbors. A coalition against him was formed by Ariarathes

V of Cappadocia, Attalus II of Pergamum and Ptolemy V of Egypt. The latter, in the name of one Alexander, pretended son of Antiochus IV, invaded Palestine and Phoenicia. Demetrius sent off into safety his two sons Demetrius and Antiochus, and then turned to face his enemies. At first successful, he eventually was overcome by superior numbers and the defection of his own troops, and died fighting bravely to the last (150 B.C.).

Figure 17.

Figure 18.

Demetrius' coins are far from rare and give us a lifelike portrait of this interesting man. His was a strong, handsome face but with a beaklike nose, (Fig. 17) which was obviously the progenitor of that oversized feature so characteristic of some of Demetrius' descendants. During the last five years of his reign a too highly idealized portrait was introduced on the issues of Antioch (Fig. 18). The reverse types chosen by Demetrius are new, representing a play upon his name. The tetradrachms usually have a seated female, variously described as Tyche or Demeter; while the drachms have the cornucopiae which on the larger coins the goddess holds in her left arm. Many of the coins struck elsewhere than in Antioch retain the reverse type of the seated Apollo.

Alexander I (150 — 145 B.C.) now reigned in Antioch, but soon gave himself up to a wild life of pleasure and debauchery. To the numismatist his coins are far more interesting than his history. On their obverses they show us a young man with regular and comely features, slightly marred however, by a jaw that is just a little too heavy. For Antioch the reverses

large series of attractive coins (Fig. 20) struck in the Phoenician cities of Berytus, Sidon, Tyre and Ake-Ptolemais. These prove what a large influence Ptolemy maintained over his protégé, for whereas all Seleucid coins had previously been of Attic weight, these are now of Phoenician weight in order to facilitate the trade with Egypt. In addition, on their reverses they bear the Ptolemaic eagle, which only serves to emphasize the preponderant commercial and political domination now enjoyed by the land of the Nile.

In the meanwhile, Demetrius II, son of Demetrius I, had managed to collect a band of mercenaries and to invade Cilicia and eastern Syria. Ptolemy VI, for his part, had become thoroughly disgusted with Alexander and now entered Palestine to support the claims of Demetrius. The allies seized Antioch and eventually defeated Alexander in a pitched battle outside the walls. Alexander fled to an Arab chieftain, who however as-

Figure 19.

Figure 20.

again return to the seated Apollo type (Fig. 19). Very important was the

Figure 21.

sassinated him; and Demetrius II ruled at Antioch. A very handsome series of dated tetradrachms (Fig. 21) was issued from that mint, while the Phoenician issues were continued at Sidon and Tyre in the name of the new king (Fig. 22).

Figure 22.

It was not long before the boundless exactions and insensate reprisals instituted by Demetrius had made him extremely unpopular. A violent insurrection broke out at Antioch, in which thousands perished and the greater part of the city was reduced to ashes. A more serious rebellion, also, was fomented by a former general, Diodotus Tryphon, who proclaimed as king the infant Antiochus, son of Alexander Bala. Demetrius was driven out of Antioch, but continued to maintain himself in Phoenicia.

Figure 23.

Figure 24.

Very attractive coins were at once struck at Antioch in the name of the youthful Antiochus: tetradrachms

with the reverse type of the galloping Dioscuri (Fig. 23), drachms with the seated Apollo (Fig. 24). The mints of Berytus, Sidon and Tyre still struck in the name of Demetrius.

The fratricidal warfare continued for a time, to the sole profit of the Jews, who under Jonathan and Simon Maccabee — by playing one side off against the other — recovered the virtual independence of Judaea and secured the coveted right of coinage.

In the meanwhile Mithradates I of Parthia had overrun Media, Persis and Elymais, and was now invading Babylonia. Demetrius II hastened to retrieve what he could of his eastern possessions, was at first successful in several battles, but eventually fell into an ambush, was captured, and honorably interned by Mithradates in distant Hyrcania. Thus relieved of the close presence of the rightful king, Tryphon became bolder, contrived the murder of the infant Antiochus (140 B.C.), and made himself king. He now struck coins (Fig. 25) in

Figure 25.

his own name and bearing the title ΒΑΣΙΛΕΩΣ ΤΡΥΦΩΝΟΣ ΑΥΤΟΚΡΑΤΟΡΟΣ thus announcing to the world that his power rested on his own might. These coins bear the interesting type of Tryphon's helmet adorned in front with a mighty horn.

The usurper, however, did not last long. It will be remembered that the second son of Demetrius I had also been sent away into safety by his careful father. In the flourishing city of Side in Pamphylia this young Antiochus had now grown to man's estate. Being of strong character and endowed with considerable native ability, he decided to make a bid for his rightful heritage. He appeared suddenly (139 B.C.) in Syria where the people, outraged by Tryphon's misdeeds, flocked to the new standard. The usurper was driven from refuge to refuge, and finally despairing of his cause, committed suicide. Antiochus VII Sidetes now reigned alone over what was left of the Seleucid kingdom. His first act was to marry Cleopatra Thea, daughter of Ptolemy VI, who had in turn been the wife of Alexander I and then of Demetrius II. To Antiochus she eventually presented no fewer than five sons.

Figure 26.

Antiochus VII's coins are quite common. In large numbers and on the Attic standard they were issued from the mints of Tarsus, Antioch and Damascus. Phoenician tetradrachms and didrachms, with the eagle reverse, were also coined at Sidon and Tyre. The portraits reveal in Antiochus his family's good looks and show him endowed with the large nose inherited from his father Demetrius I. The reverse types of the Attic tetradrachms have a standing Athena (referring, probably, to the patron goddess of Side where the young man had for so many years found a safe refuge) or, for Tarsus, the Pyre of Sandan (Fig. 26). The drachms, with more than usual historical correctness, bear the figure of victory.

In the nine years of his able reign Antiochus brought a certain amount of recovery and prosperity to the harassed kingdom. By 130 B.C. he felt himself strong enough to measure swords with Parthia, now ruled by Mithradates' son Phraates II. Antiochus at the head of a powerful army invaded Mesopotamia, was successful in several battles and had recovered Babylonia and Media when he was overtaken by winter. He went into winter quarters at Ecbatana and distributed his army throughout the surrounding province. But the Parthian king was not idle and perfected his deep laid plans. A vast conspiracy was formed among the inhabitants of Media, and, just before the opening of spring, on an appointed day, the whole province rose and massacred the scattered forces of Antiochus. Phraates himself advanced upon Ecbatana with his main army, the while he set free the imprisoned Demetrius II in order that the latter might raise a revolt in Antiochus' rear. The few forces which the Syrian king still had about him were routed, and Antiochus himself either fell on the field of battle or perished by his own hand. The Syrian army was completely annihilated and the Parthians recovered everything, as far as the Euphrates.

Meanwhile Demetrius had safely reached Antioch, and once more commenced to strike money with his own name and portrait. But his long sojourn among the Parthians had had its effect and his coins of Attic weight henceforth bear a portrait with a flowing beard (Fig. 27). At Tyre, however, the beardless portrait of former years was still continued.

Figure 27.

In 129 B.C. Demetrius essayed an attack on Egypt and had progressed as far as Pelusium when a revolt broke out at Antioch. A certain Alexander, who gave himself out as a son of Bala, had proclaimed himself king (128 B.C.). Demetrius hurried back from Egypt, but was completely routed by the usurper in a battle near Damascus. He fled to Ptolemais where resided his former wife Cleôpatra Thea, but she closed the gates against him. Demetrius had no better success at Tyre, and was finally captured and executed.

Figure 28.

Coins of Alexander II, nicknamed Zebina (128—123 B.C.), are known for Tarsus, Antioch and Damascus. At the Cilician mint the reverse type is the usual Pyre of Sandan, while the issues of the other mints have a seated Zeus (Fig. 28).

When the redoubtable Cleopatra shut the gates of Ptolemais in the face of her quondam husband, she decided herself to assume the reins of government. She did away with her oldest son by Antiochus VII, named Seleucus (V), and struck some extremely rare tetradrachms bearing her own portrait. Sensing perhaps that public opinion was still too strongly against the sole rule of a woman, Cleopatra in 125 B.C. associated with herself on the throne her next oldest son Antiochus, now the eighth of that name. He was popularly known as Grypus, because of his enormous, beaklike nose which, doubtless, represented an inheritance from his grandfather, Demetrius I.

Coins were struck in the joint names of mother and son, first at Ptolemais, then (after the death of Zebina) at Tarsus, Antioch, Damas-

Figure 29.

cus and Sidon. Tyre no longer issued royal money, having secured her freedom in 126 B.C. and inaugurated her own coinage with autonomous types and dates. The other coins now bear Cleopatra's bust, her hair in long ringlets and adorned with an impressive diadem — while from behind her masterful profile peers forth the youthful face of Grypus with his large, curving nose (Fig. 29). The reverse types are as usual: Pyre of Sandan for

[73]

Tarsus; seated Zeus for Antioch, Damascus and Ptolemais; eagle for Sidon.

Figure 30.

When Alexander II had finally been overcome and destroyed, there no longer existed any dangerous rivals. Cleopatra was apparently loath to continue playing second fiddle to her growing son, and attempted to poison him. But Antiochus was on his guard and forced his mother to drink the cup prepared for himself (121 B.C.). For the next ten years the coins bear only his portrait, while on the reverses we see, at first, a standing Athena, later a standing figure of the Celestial Zeus — Zeus Ouranios — holding a large star in his outstretched right (Fig. 30).

In the meanwhile there had grown up at Cyzicus Antiochus' younger brother, also named Antiochus, but popularly known as Cyzicenus from his place of abode. This young man now made a bid for sovereignty by gathering a force of mercenaries and suddenly invading Syria (113 B.C.). Partial success crowned his efforts and he secured Antioch. There ensued an intermittent and long drawn out struggle for supremacy between the two brothers, first one and then the other gaining the upper hand. The interchanging vicissitudes of the strife can be followed clearly in their several coinages.

Each brother, at one time or another, held such cities as Tarsus, Antioch, Damascus or Ptolemais where they struck coins which are frequently

Figure 31.

dated. Those of Grypus have already been briefly described. Those of Cyzicenus bear on their obverses his youthful portrait, wearing a slight beard and side-whiskers; on their reverses they have a standing figure of Athena (Fig. 31) in imitation of the coins of his father Antiochus VII Sidetes. The official epithet always employed by Grypus is Epiphanes, by Cyzicenus Philopator.

Through mutual exhaustion, a truce seems eventually to have taken place — Grypus ruling in Antioch, Cyzicenus in Phoenicia. About 108—

Figure 32.

7 B.C. the former changed the reverse type of his tetradrachms from Zeus Ouranios to the seated Zeus Nicephorus (Fig. 32). This type was continued until the death of Grypus in 96 B.C.

Antiochus IX Cyzicenus at once reoccupied Antioch, and thence issued a new series of coins (Fig. 33) which now bear his clean-shaven portrait, while the seated Zeus of the reverse

Figure 33.

is taken over from the final coinage of his dead brother. In fact, the seated Zeus, surrounded by a laurel wreath, remains (except for a short period under the rule of Tigranes of Armenia) the invariable reverse type of the silver coinages of Antioch until Augustus changed it again about the year 7 B.C.

Cyzicenus did not long survive his brother but died in 95 B.C. while engaged in a campaign against the eldest of Grypus' sons, Seleucus VI. The latter at once entered Antioch, and the coins of that city now in turn, bear his characteristic profile (Fig. 34). We can recognize, once more, the large,

Figure 34.

curved, ancestral nose, as well as an expression which supports Appian's description of his character as "the most violent and tyrranical possible."

Cyzicenus had left one son who, with the help of a courtesan, had escaped from Antioch and sought refuge in Aradus. He now gathered some forces together, advanced on Antioch, drove out Seleucus, pursued him into

Figure 35.

Cilicia, and again defeated him near Mopsuestia. Seleucus threw himself into that city, but perished in a popular uprising when he tried to raise a large sum of money from the reluctant citizens (95 B.C.). Antiochus X now reigned in Antioch for a brief space, and struck the usual tetradrachms provided with his portrait. (Fig. 35.)

Figure 36.

Of the five sons left by Grypus the oldest was now dead, but the next two, the twins Antiochus and Philip, took up the quarrel, avenged the death of their brother on Mopsuestia, and then advanced and captured Antioch from their cousin Antiochus X. The elder of the twins, Antiochus XI, had just time to strike a few very rare coins (Fig. 36) before Antiochus X returned and drove him out again. In his flight he perished while attempting to swim the Orontes.

In the meanwhile the fourth brother, Demetrius, had established himself in Damascus with the aid of Ptolemy Lathyrus, king of Cyprus. As Demetrius III he reigned there for

Figure 37.

just short of ten years, during which time he struck some interesting dated tetradrachms (Fig. 37), with his bearded portrait on the obverse and a strange representation of the Syrian goddess Atergatis of Damascus on the reverse.

Antiochus X continued his reign at Antioch for a little time longer, and is then said to have perished (about 92 B.C.) in a battle against the Parthians. Demetrius III thereupon appears to have secured Antioch, for a short space indeed, but long enough to strike there a few exceedingly rare tetradrachms of the Antiochene type. Philip returned at this juncture, recovered Antioch and relegated his brother to Damascus.

The Antiochene issues of Philip (Fig. 38) must have been enormous.

Figure 38.

So widespread and popular did they become that years after, under the Romans, they were imitated over a long period, until Augustus finally put an end to them, about 12 B.C.

The strife between Philip and Demetrius III continued merrily along. The capture of the latter by the Parthians (87 B.C.) made little difference, for his place was at once taken by the last of the five brothers, Antiochus XII, who divided his time between fighting Philip, harassing the Jews and attacking the Nabataeans. He finally perished in a battle with the latter (84 B.C.), leaving us some very rare tetradrachms with the interesting reverse type of the great god Haddad of Damascus.

By 83 B.C. the people of Syria had become so utterly fed up with the interminable fratricidal wars of these last miserable scions of the Seleucid line that, in desperation, they sought the protection of Tigranes of Armenia and joyfully hailed him as their king. Fourteen years of comparative peace did Tigranes give them, though, by the end of that time, they had grown heartily sick of him too. For the coins which Tigranes struck at Antioch and Damascus see the chapter which deals with the coinages of the Armenian kings.

The Seleucid series, nevertheless, does not end here, for there still existed in exile the young son of Antiochus X, also named Antiochus. When Lucullus had defeated Tigranes in 69 B.C. and forced him out of Syria, Antiochus XIII recovered the throne of his ancestors, with the consent of the Syrians themselves. Possessing little ability and fewer resources the young man proved himself but the shadow of a king. It was not long before the country was in a turmoil again, which was only put an end to when Pompey the Great arrived in 64 B.C., rearranged the affairs of the East, and made of Syria a Roman province. Antiochus was shortly after murdered by an Arab emir into whose clutches he had fallen.

On the few coins that survive of Antiochus XIII (Fig. 39) we behold the portrait of a somewhat fatuous young man; though endowed with the large Seleucid nose, this feature seems unable to redeem the utterly vacuous expression possessed by this last feeble descendant of a very long and picturesque line of kings.

Figure 39.

FOURTEEN

THE GREEK KINGS
OF BACTRIA

THE handsome coins of the Greek kings of Bactria have always enjoyed high renown among both collectors and scholars, because of their excellent artistic qualities and their great historical value. To the meagre sources of information, culled from casual references here and there in the work of two or three ancient writers, these coins offer not only definite confirmation but also add the names and portraits of otherwise completely forgotten rulers. And what portraits they are! They possess not only the purely objective and brutal frankness of later Roman portraiture, but to this they add that spiritual quality, that revelation of the inner soul and character of the subject which only Greek artists seemed able to secure.

So far as the history is concerned, we know that towards the close of the troubled reign of the Seleucid king Antiochus II, Diodotus, satrap of Bactria, revolted and secured his independence. Scholars are agreed that this event took place about 250 B.C., or very shortly after. Bactria was at that time one of the richest and most flourishing provinces of the empire. It covered a vast extent of territory, comprising what is now northern Afghanistan as well as the districts of Merv, Bokhara and Samarcand. It was endowed with immense resources in fruitful fields and rich pastures, was very populous, and was said to have boasted no less than a thousand cities.

Ancient historians infer that Diodotus did not long survive his revolt and was succeeded by his son of the same

Figure 1.

Figure 2.

name. The first coins, staters and tetradrachms (Fig. 1), which we can assign to the new dynasty bear indeed the name of Antiochus, but the diademed portrait is that of Diodotus and the thundering Zeus on the reverse is not a Seleucid type at all but the canting badge of Diodotus. These coins did not last very long and are replaced by exactly similar staters (Fig. 2) and tetradrachms provided with the name of Diodotus himself.

Diodotus II certainly continued to reign until after about 237 B.C., at which time we know he was engaged in repulsing an attack by Seleucus II. Thereupon complete darkness descends over the Bactrian district and lasts until the famous eastern expedition of Antiochus III. At that time (about 208 B.C.) we find ruling over Bactria a certain Euthydemus, a native of Magnesia on the Hermus. How he got to Bactria, or by what steps he rose to a position from which he could successfully grasp at the supreme power, we do not know. Be that as it may, we read that Antiochus by a ruse crossed the frontier river of the Harirud, and on the other side won a hard fought cavalry battle. Euthydemus withdrew to his capital Zariaspa (modern Balkh) where he concentrated his main army to face Antiochus. The ensuing struggle was long and indecisive, time was pressing, while the barbarian tribes on the northern frontier were becoming restive and threatening. Eventually negotiations for peace were inaugurated, to the success of which Euthydemus' handsome and prepossessing son Demetrius contributed not a little. Antiochus was completely won over by the young man, terms honorable and advantageous to both sides were ratified, and the daughter of the Syrian king affianced to Demetrius. Thence Antiochus and his army moved on to their conquests in Afghanistan and India, leaving Euthydemus the acknowledged ruler of Bactria.

Figure 3.

As the coins of Euthydemus are not rare, and as they reveal considerable variation in portraiture, style, fabric

and monograms, they suggest a reign of some duration. While the tetradrachm pictured in Fig. 3 portrays a

Figure 4.

man in middle life, Fig. 4 gives us a truly remarkable presentation of an elderly man of many experiences and great force of character. The reverse type is always a seated Heracles, imitated from certain Seleucid coins of western Asia Minor, with which coins Euthydemus must have been well familiar in his early youth.

Even before the death of his father, Demetrius had probably embarked upon that career of conquest which still echoes faintly from a single sentence of Justin and — of all places — from the deathless verse of Chaucer. Well would we like to believe that some now-perished manuscript had furnished the English poet with his vivid description of

"The great Emetrius, the King of Ind"
who
" Upon a steedé bay, trapped in steel,
Covered with clothe of gold, diápred wele
Came riding like the God of Armes,
Mars."

Dryden has successfully modernized the remainder into:
" His amber-colored locks in ringlets run
With graceful negligence, and shone against the sun;
His nose was aquiline, his eyes were blue;

Ruddy his lips, and fair and fresh his
hue,
Some sprinkled freckles on his face were
seen
Whose dusk set off the whiteness of the
skin."

Figure 5.

His coins remain today the only proof positive that we possess of Demetrius' Indian conquests. But they speak in no uncertain terms. On their obverses (Fig. 5) we may still behold an extraordinarily spirited portrait of the Indian conqueror, symbolized by the elephant's head-dress which crowns his brow. On the reverses the resting Heracles of Euthydemus' coins has now arisen, and with youthful vigor faces the beholder and proudly places upon his own brow the wreath of victory.

Figure 6.

Demetrius apparently left two sons, one of the same name ruling in Bac-

tria; the other, named Euthydemus after his grandfather, ruling further south — perhaps in the districts about modern Kabul, Ghazni, or Kandahar. The coins of Demetrius II are found only in Bactria and Persia, and as they are very rare indeed his reign must have been quite brief. The coins of Euthydemus II (Fig. 6) go those of his father one better — not only does Heracles stand facing, with a wreath upon his head, but he actually holds another wreath in his right hand.

Figure 7.

This prince was very shortly followed by two others, father and son to judge by their portraits, who bear the names of Pantaleon and Agathocles. Their silver coins, provided with the same monograms as those of Euthydemus II, are exceedingly rare. Fortunately for collectors, their copper coins are fairly common. Square, after the Indian fashion, they bear an interesting representation of some goddess holding a flower and clad in oriental costume with trousers (Fig. 7). Older students have recognized in this figure a dancing nautch girl! Of even more interest to us is the fact that the three last named kings also struck coins in copper-nickel, the first recorded use of that metal for coinage purposes, and not again employed until quite recent times.

The immediate successor to Agathocles was one Antimachus, whose astonishingly modern portrait, wearing a sort of Scottish tam-o-shanter, sug-

Figure 8.

gests a person full of humor and bonhomie (Fig. 8). The reverse type appears to be a diademed Poseidon, holding a trident and a filleted palm branch. A victorious Poseidon, on coins from inland Afghanistan or northwestern India, has given scholars many headaches to explain. But, after all, the figure may only be a graecicised version of some Indian deity, such as Siva, who regularly carries a trident.

drachms bearing on their obverses what, according to the accompanying inscriptions, purported to be portraits of Alexander the son of Philip, Antiochus (II), Diodotus, Euthydemus (Fig 9), and Demetrius. These portraits are accompanied, each by their respective reverse types, but now with the inscription ΒΑΣΙΛΕΥΟΝΤΟΣ ΑΓΑΘΟΚΛΕΟΥΣ ΔΙΚΑΙΟΥ or ΒΑΣΙΛΕ-ΥΟΝΤΟΣ ΑΝΤΙΜΑΧΟΥ ΘΕΟΥ (Fig. 9), as the case may be. These rather unique coins evidently served the purpose of political manifestos, struck and circulated to proclaim what Agathocles and Antimachus wished the world to think was their legal heritage by which they claimed their right to rule. The coins presuppose the existence of some dangerous rival challenging this "right." Who may this suppositious rival have been? None other than the great Eucratides, who is supposed to have rebelled against Demetrius and who, as Justin tells us, fought many wars and

Figure 9.

Figure 10.

Both Agathocles and Antimachus struck a curious but very instructive set of medals or propaganda tetra-

in the end conquered India. He, too, struck commemorative coins (Fig. 10) designed to establish HIS claim to the throne and be a counterblast to the propaganda issues of his opponents.

On the obverse of these coins we see the jugate busts of an elderly man and a woman who, the accompanying inscription tells us, are Heliocles and Laodice. On the reverse is the characteristic portrait of Eucratides himself, wearing diadem and crested helmet. Now Heliocles is bare-headed, while Laodice is adorned with the royal diadem. Obviously the two busts on the obverse represent the parents of Eucratides who thus claimed his right to the throne through descent from Laodice the daughter (or, possibly, the widow?) of Diodotus, Euthydemus or Demetrius.

by his son, who then ruled in his stead. Unfortunately the imbecilic Justin neglects to mention the son's name.

Figure 12.

Figure 13.

Figure 11.

The ordinary types of the coins of Eucratides have for the obverse his diademed or helmeted (Fig. 11) bust to r.; for the reverse a spirited scene of the charging Dioscuri. These coins are comparatively common, and were widely struck, in Bactria, Afghanistan and India.

Justin also tells us that on his return from his Indian conquests, Eucratides was cold-bloodedly murdered

It may have been another Eucratides (Fig. 12), or Heliocles (Fig. 13), both of whom struck coins, the one with a standing Apollo on the reverse, the other with a facing Zeus. These are apparently the last Greek coins of Bactria, for shortly after, circa 135 B.C., the Saka tribes burst over the northern boundary and inundated Bactria. Thus was extinguished at last that splendid Greek kingdom which had enjoyed a glorious, though somewhat agitated existence for upwards of a hundred years.

FIFTEEN

THE GREEK KINGS
OF INDIA

IF THE existing literary records of the Greek kings of Bactria are pitifully scant, those of their successors in India may be said to be almost nonexistent. We possess only three short notices. Strabo mentions the fact that a certain Menander conquered more provinces in India than did even Alexander the Great; Plutarch recounts the story that after Menander's death the cities of his realm contended for the honor of preserving his ashes; while the writer of the Periplus of the Erythraean Sea states that in his day (about 150 A.D.) the coins of Apollodotus and Menander were still current in the bazaars of Barygaza, the modern Broach near Baroda. Barring a few very vague references to invading Greeks in native Indian sources, and the Buddhist treatise known as the Milindapañha or "Questions of Milinda (= Menander)," there survives nothing more. The continued existence of numerous successors to Demetrius and Eucratides in India has been totally forgotten by history. Only their coins remain today, inciting our imagination to weave the romantic story of these far away Hellenes, completely cut off from their kinsmen in the West and destined eventually to be submerged by the rising tides of the native populations by which they were surrounded.

We have learned, in the preceding chapter, that Eucratides was succeeded in Bactria by two more rulers, one

of whom was Heliocles. The latter also struck coins (Fig. 1) in the Kabul Valley. These coins now bear bilingual

Figure 1.

inscriptions (Greek and Kharoshti), and are no longer of Attic weight but based on the Persic or Indian system. That system had already been adopted by both Demetrius and Eucratides probably just before their death, so rare are the existing specimens. The system had indeed actually been in use in India long before the coming of Alexander. Some scholars even believe that it antidates the Persian domination. Be that as it may, it had become thoroughly *enraciné* among the Indian peoples, and its adoption, together with bilingual inscriptions, by the Greek kings is the first evident sign of their complete separation from the West.

Figure 2.

Alongside of Heliocles there existed other rulers. To the south, around

Kandahar, was Apollodotus Soter (Fig. 2) who at first employed the Attic system for his hemidrachms, to be

Figure 3.

Figure 4.

followed by square drachms of Indian weight. He was ruling even before the death of Eucratides, for we possess copper coins of the latter restruck on those of Apollodotus. To the east, in Taxila, there ruled one Antialcidas, a powerful king who has left us many tetradrachms (Fig. 3) and drachms (Fig. 4), as well as the only extant royal Greek inscription in India — the now famous pillar of Besnagar. This was set up by Heliodorus, son of Dion, Antialcidas' ambassador to the king of Vidica (Bhilsa). The elephant appearing with Zeus on the reverses of Antialcidas' coins proclaim his conquests over Indian peoples.

Figure 5.

Heliocles and Apollodotus were succeeded in Afghanistan by a number of princes: Strato I (Fig. 5), Archebius

Figure 6.

(Fig. 6), Polyxenus, Peucolaus, Amyntas (Fig. 7) and Hermaeus (Fig. 8). The last of these must have enjoyed a comparatively long reign, as his

Figure 7.

Figure 8.

coins are very numerous and reveal a gradual falling off in style. With the exception of the last mentioned coins, the issues of these rulers are still of remarkably fine style. Their varied portraits are extraordinarily life-like and redolent of the Greek genius. Each of the kings had his own reverse type: Heliocles the standing Zeus; Strato the fighting Athena; Archebius the thundering Zeus, facing; Peucolaus Zeus standing to l. with sceptre; Amyntas the fighting Athena interchanging with the enthroned Zeus; Hermaeus the seated "Mithra," rayed and wearing the so-called "Phrygian" cap.

The Greek kings in Afghanistan were gradually hemmed in and their territories one by one cut off by the surrounding Barbarians. In the south and west encroached the Sakas, spreading southwards from their Bactrian conquests. The earliest of their princes, one Maues, employs on his coins the same monogram as had previously appeared on certain issues of Heliocles, Strato I, Polyxenus, Archebius and Amyntas. The later copper coins, bearing the types of Hermaeus, were copied by the Kushan prince Kadphises after he had burst through the mountain barrier of the Hindu Kush on the north.

Figure 9.

Figure 10.

In India proper, that is in Gandhara, around Taxila and the modern Peshawer, Antialcidas was followed by Lysias (Fig. 9), Diomed (Fig. 10), Philoxenus (Fig. 11), Nicias (Fig. 12) and Theophilus. The territories of two of these kings, Diomed and Philoxenus, seem for a time to have extended

further to the west, because some of the monograms on their coins are identical with those found on the

Figure 11.

Figure 12.

coins of the "Afghan" Greeks. On the other hand, for all that we can say now, the situation may have been reversed and the latter may once have held lands to the east of Afghanistan, which they later lost to the Gandhara Greeks. These princes, too, vary their reverse types. Lysias copies the coins of Demetrius, Diomed takes over the Dioscuri from the coins of Eucratides, while Philoxenus depicts himself, helmeted and fully accoutered, on a prancing horse to r. Nicias, on his unique tetradrachm, displays the fighting Athena, while on his drachms he depicts himself standing in armor and holding a palm branch. With the exception of many of Philoxenus' is-

Figure 13.

sues, the style of these coins is still quite good, the portraiture excellent.

Over the territories once ruled by these princes eventually swept the power of the great Menander (Fig. 13). From native sources we learn that he had been born at Alexandria sub Caucaso, the modern Charsadda; that he later became king of Cakala (Sialkot) that he was mighty in wealth, prosperity and the number of his armed hosts; that he was as wise as he was strong of body, swift and valorous; and that he became deeply interested in Buddhism, to which he was finally converted. His coins tell us that he succeeded one Antimachus Nicephorus, who may or may not have been the same person as the Antimachus Theos mentioned as among the Bactrian Greeks. Menander's extremely common coins, adorned with the fighting Athena, attest his power, the length of his reign and the width of his dominions.

Figure 14.

After Menander's death, his territories were parceled out among numerous contending rivals. First Zoilus (Fig. 14) struck some drachms of fine style, with his diademed portrait on the obverse and on the reverse a standing Heracles copied from the coins of Euthydemus II. He was soon relegated, however, to the eastern portions of his heritage (the Sialkot district?) where he continued to strike drachms, of rapidly deteriorating

style, with the fighting Athena on the reverse.

Figure 15.

Further west, Epander (Fig. 15) and Apollodotus II (Fig. 16) secured portions of Menander's realms and struck coins with Menander's reverse type of the fighting Athena. Epander soon disappeared, but Apollodotus seems to have been more successful, and his coins are plentiful. He even overcame, or succeeded Zoilus in the

Figure 16.

Figure 17.

Figure 18.

east and continued to issue coins there. In that district he was eventually succeeded by Dionysus, followed by Strato II (Fig. 17) and Apollophanes (Fig. 18), who all struck debased drachms of very poor style. With the last named, Greek domination comes to an end here and we then find similar drachms of the Saka king Ranjubula.

Figure 19.

In the meanwhile, one Artemidorus had carved out a kingdom for himself in the mountains to the north. He took over one of Hermaeus' mints and struck many coins (Fig. 19) with his diademed portrait on the obverse, and Nike or the hunting Artemis on the reverse.

Figure 20.

But by this time Greek rule had also drawn to a close in Gandhara. The coins of Apollodotus had grown somewhat cruder, as time went on, though they never entirely lost a certain Greek quality in their style and die-cutting. His immediate successor was Hippostratus whose coins (Fig. 20) continue the style and monograms of Apollodotus, though with changed reverse types. He chose either the standing figure of Tyche, or the armed horseman of Philoxenus, sometimes prancing, sometimes standing still and raising his right arm as if in the act of haranguing his army. But now the Sakas, having conquered all southern Afghanistan, forced their way into India proper. The same Maues, who had previously occupied the mints and carried on the coinages of Amyntas, now secures one of Hippostratus' mints — as well as of the obscure Telephus, known to us only by one or two extremely rare coins. The successors of Maues, Azes and Azilises, finally overcame Hippostratus, occupied his last mints, and superseded his coinages with their own.

Thus comes to a close the glorious but tragic rule of the last of Alexander's successors in India. Step by step the numismatist is enabled, by their coins, to follow the romantic story of this little island of Hellenic people lost in the distant East. Surrounded on all sides, completely cut off from any help from their western kinsmen, they succumbed at last, as needs must be, to superior numbers and to that inherent Greek trait of fierce independence, which makes it impossible for them to unite for any length of time, even in the face of the direst danger. None the less, by their brilliant abilities and the fighting qualities inherited from their Macedonian ancestors, they had for a time held aloft the torch of Hellenic culture in an alien land, and amidst a vastly more numerous people.

SIXTEEN

THE PARTHIAN
KINGS

ABOUT the year 250 B.C. the nomad tribe of the Dahae, residing in the province of Parthia, under their chieftain Arsaces revolted from Seleucid rule and proclaimed their independence. Arsaces died shortly afterwards and it was his brother Tiridates I (248-211 B.C.) who finally established the Parthian power and founded their capital at Dara. Little is known concerning the succeeding princes, Arsaces, Phriapatius and Phraates I, except that the first of these sustained with difficulty the attack of Antiochus III, but that under his successors the territory then lost was gradually recovered.

To Phraates I succeeded his brother Mithradates I in 171 B.C., and under his able rule the kingdom of Parthia rapidly expanded. In the East several provinces were wrested from the Bactrian king Eucratides. In the West Media was overrun, Babylonia was invaded and its capital Seleucia captured, and finally Elymais (Susiana) was subjugated. At the death of Mithradates the Parthian territory stretched from the Euphrates to the Hindu Kush.

The earliest Parthian coins are

drachms (Fig. 1) bearing on the obverse the beardless head of Arsaces, wearing the Scytho-Persian bonnet, well known and still much used in modern Turkey. On the reverse is rep-

Figure 2.

resented the divine founder of the dynasty, the first Arsaces, in Scythian costume with cap, mantle, and trousers, seated on the omphalos and holding a bow in his outstretched right. Some of these coins may have been struck by the predecessors of Mithradates I, but the majority probably date from the commencement of his reign. Soon, however, the bearded, diademed bust of Mithradates replaces (Fig. 2) the bonnetted head — the reverse type and inscription remaining

Figure 1.

Figure 3.

the same. When Mithradates had added Media to his realms he struck in Ecbatana, the capital of his new province, tetradrachms (Fig. 3) of Greek style and modeled after the coins of his contemporary Demetrius I of Syria. On the fall of Seleucia, that city's mint continued to operate for its new lord and master and struck some handsome, dated tetradrachms

Figure 4.

(Fig. 4) with a standing Heracles on the reverse, accompanied by an inscription which vaunts the Philhellenism of Mithradates. This policy, first openly avowed by Mithradates and continued by most of his successors, was intended to conciliate the teeming populace of the great metropolis, who jealously guarded and maintained their Greek heritage of city institutions, laws and language.

To Mithradates I there succeeded in 137/6 B.C. his son Phraates II. Though he temporarily lost Babylonia and Media to Antiochus VII, in 129 B.C., he annihilated the Syrian king, together with his army, and regained all of his lost provinces. He perished in 128/7 B.C., whilst fighting Scythian invaders in the eastern portions of his kingdom. Phraates II, to judge by his coins (Figs. 5, 6), lacked the high-bridged, aristocratic nose, the noble beard and dignified bearing

Figure 6.

of his father. His tetradrachms, for the most part, are after the Greek model, with a seated, bearded, Asiatic Dionysus, in long flowing robes, seated enthroned on the reverse. The title Nikephorus and the victory in Dionysus' hand prove that these coins were struck after the great victory over

Figure 7.

Antiochus. The accompanying, rare drachms also have a standing figure of the winged victory on their re-

Figure 5.

verses. Phraates' usual drachms, however, have the accustomed Parthian type of the seated Arsaces (Fig. 6).

His uncle Artabanus I (128/7 - 123 B.C.) succeeded him, but also perished fighting the bellicose Scythians. Artabanus, in turn, possesses the fine and dignified features of his brother Mithradates I. His dated tetradrachms (Fig. 7), probably struck in Seleucia, are Greek in type and style; while his drachms follow the usual Parthian model.

In 123 B.C. the great Mithradates II, son of Artabanus I, succeeded his father on the throne. Justin tells us that by his achievements he earned the surname "great"; he checked the advance of the Scythians and "added many peoples to the realm of Parthia." Commensurate with his long reign, as with the wide extent and power of his kingdom, the coins of Mithradates II are numerous.

Figure 8.

The tetradrachms (Fig. 8) now assume a more oriental aspect. The king's bust is clothed in an embroidered robe, perhaps studded with pearls. The reverse follows the type of the drachms, with the seated Arsaces figure and the box-like arrangement of the inscription. As Mithradates ad-

vances in years his beard grows longer and the titles he assumes more grandiloquent. About half way through

Figure 9.

his reign he adopts (Fig. 9) the typical oriental designation, hallowed by countless ages — "Great King of Kings." Soon after this he also commences to wear a most impressive headdress, a large tiara, with rounded top and long side flaps, richly embroidered with designs of crescents, stars and other devices picked out in

Figure 10.

pearls and precious stones (Fig. 10).

At Mithradates' death (about 91 B.C. ?) troublous times broke over the kingdom. Hordes of Scythians again burst into the country on the east, Tigranes of Armenia recovered large tracts of land in the west and usurped the title "King of Kings," while internecine struggles took place between the sons and relatives of the dead monarch. The person who actually succeeded Mithradates II, and struck numerous coins, is known to numismatists as "Artabanus II." He is probably, however, the Gotarzes (I) or the Orodes (I) of the clay tablets found in recent years in Babylonia. On his coins (Fig. 11) this young ruler displays the big, curved nose inherited from his father, long locks falling almost to his shoulder, and a short, clipped and carefully tended beard.

Figure 11.

The anarchy which had followed Mithradates' death was, about 77 B.C., finally put an end to by the aged Sinatruces who, Lucian says, was eighty years old when he returned from exile among the Scythians and ascended the Parthian throne. As he calls himself Autocrator on his coins, he may have assumed the power more or less through his own efforts. His large and very hawk-like nose suggests a close relationship with Mithradates II and his successor — he may have been the brother of the one and the uncle of the other. His reputed age is certainly quite obvious on his

Figure 12.

coins (Fig. 12). He adopts the embroidered tiara and the title Philhel-

Figure 13.

lene from the last issues of Mithradates II.

Sinatruces was followed by his son Phraates III about 70 B.C. In features the new ruler does not resemble his father as much as one might have expected, for though his nose is indeed large and nobly curved, it has not the extraordinary "hawkish" crook of his predecessor's. Also his beard is longer and quite untrimmed. Sometimes he appears wearing the simple diadem only (Fig. 13), at other times the high-curved tiara, whose outer rim is now ornamented

Figure 14.

with reclining stags (Fig. 14). The reverse type of one issue of his tetradrachms (Fig. 14) shows the city of Seleucia crowning the seated king, probably in commemoration of his successes over Tigranes of Armenia.

About 57 B.C. Phraates was murdered by his two precious sons, Mithradates III and Orodes, who immediately commenced to quarrel violently with each other over their ill-gotten spoils. For some three years the struggle continued with varying fortunes. At one time Mithradates was forced to flee for his life to Gabinius, the Roman proconsul of Syria. He later recovered some of his lands, but eventually lost Seleucia and surrendered to Orodes, who executed him in 54 B.C.

Thus freed of his brother's annoying presence, Orodes turned to face the Roman invasion under Crassus. At Carrhae (53 B.C.) he won his memorable victory over the Romans, who lost their commander and the bulk of their army. During the ensuing years the forces of Orodes twice invaded the Roman provinces. Once they even captured Antioch and pressed on into Cilicia and southern Asia Minor. Eventually, however, Antony's general, Ventidius Bassus, drove them out again, and in 38 B.C. decisively defeated the Parthians in the great battle of Grindarus in Cyrrhestica.

During the fratricidal struggle mentioned above, Mithradates III issued

Figure 15.

Figure 16.

two series of coins, one with his diademed bust to l. (Fig. 15), the other with the interesting and beautifully executed facing bust (Fig. 16). The latter is one of the most attractive of Parthian coins.

Throughout his reign of twenty years Orodes struck great quantities of tetradrachms and drachms, all

bearing his diademed and robed bust to l. On the drachms the bust is frequently accompanied by stars and crescents, and, once, by a winged victory to commemorate Orodes' final triumph over Mithradates. The reverse type of the drachms is always the seated Arsaces, while on the tetradrachms we find the king enthroned to r. and stretching out his hand to-

Figure 17.

wards the personification of Seleucia kneeling before him (Fig. 17). Sometimes, however, Seleucia is standing and offering to the king a palm branch as the token of victory.

Orodes, in his turn, was murdered by his son Phraates IV, who then ruled the kingdom from 38/7 to 3/2 B.C. After Marc Antony's attempt to invade Parthia had been repulsed with great loss, the two empires lived at peace with each other for many years. Very friendly relations were established with Augustus and an exchange of amenities took place. Greatly to the delight of the emperor the Roman standards, captured many years before from Crassus, were peaceably recovered and the event was commemorated innumerable times on the Roman coins of the period. Augustus presented to Phraates a beautiful slave girl, Musa by name, whom he eventually married.

Figure 18.

The Parthian kingdom recovered its prosperity under Phraates IV, as attested by the enormous quantities of coins which he issued. His drachms are very like those of Orodes, and his bust is accompanied by a wreath-bearing eagle or victory, frequently with the usual stars and crescents in addition. The reverses of his tetradrachms display the seated king, sometimes alone, sometimes receiving a wreath or palm from the tyche of Seleucia (Fig. 18) or from Athena. The king's bust is always decked out with a sumptuously embroidered robe.

Figure 19.

If, after his defeat of Antony, Phraates IV lived at peace with Rome, his reign nevertheless was plagued by internal dissensions. None proved more dangerous than the revolt engineered by Tiridates II, who seems twice to have been able to capture Seleucia and strike there some dated tetra-

drachms (Fig. 19). These coins, except for the portrait which they bear, are in general appearance not unlike the tetradrachms of Phraates himself.

Figure 20.

By the beautiful but unscrupulously ambitious Musa, Phraates had a son, usually called Phraataces (Fig. 20). He and his charming mother, growing weary of waiting for the old king to die, eventually contrived to murder him. On his coins Phraates V (Phraataces) greatly resembles his father, but his head is frequently accompanied by two victories. His usual reverse type, for both tetradrachms and drachms, is the accustomed seated Arsaces holding a bow. But there is one exceptionally interesting issue (Figs. 21, 22) which bears the portrait of the celebrated, if infamous, Musa

Figure 21.

Figure 22.

instead. The queen wears a diadem with flying ends, earrings, jeweled clasp, necklace and, last but not least, a very extraordinary crown, built up in several tiers and adorned with pearls and precious stones — the like of which is not found elsewhere, unless it be the Papal tiara. Accompanying this interesting type is the welcome inscription ΘΕΑΣ ΟΥΡΑΝΙΑΣ ΜΟΥΣΗΣ ΒΑΣΙΛΙΣ-ΣΗΣ. Thus we are certain that we see before us the "Goddess Urania, Queen Musa," in other words, the glorified slave girl sent by Augustus, who became the queen of Parthia, the murderess of her husband and is later said by Josephus even to have married her own son, Phraataces!

The fall of Phraataces was brought about in 4 A.D. by a revolt of the Parthian nobles. There then ensued a period of trouble and anarchy until in 8 A.D. an embassy was sent to Rome requesting Augustus to allow the return of one of the four sons of Phraates IV, long held as hostages. The eldest, Vonones, was chosen, but because of his western manners, his effeminacy and his dislike for the manly Parthian sport of riding and hunting, he soon lost the respect and loyalty of his subjects. A rival soon arose in the person of Artabanus II who possessed all the virtues admired by the Parthians, having been brought up among the nomadic Dahae. In the

first encounter the troops of Vonones triumphed, and interesting tetra-

Figure 24.

drachms (Fig. 23) and drachms (Fig. 24) were struck celebrating this success. A large figure of victory constitutes the reverse type and, lest there be any mistake, she is accompanied on the drachms by the inscription ΒΑCΙΛΕΥC ΟΝΩΝΗC ΝΕΙΚΗCΑC ΑΡΤΑΒΑΝΟΝ: "King Vonones victorious over Artabanus." Would that all Parthian kings had been so thoughtful of posterity as to employ such explicit inscriptions!

But Artabanus was not discouraged by this setback, and four years later returned and finally ousted Vonones. He then struck dated tetradrachms of the usual type with Tyche handing a palm to the seated king. In 26/7 A.D. Artabanus introduced completely new and rather striking designs for his tetradrachms (Fig. 25) — constituting the last flare up of any originality or

Figure 25.

Figure 23.

[94]

artistic ability among Parthian die-cutters. On the obverse we see the robed, bearded, long-haired, diademed bust of the king in full face to the front. On the reverse Tyche is standing with sceptre and palm, greeting the mounted king advancing left, his r. arm raised to receive the palm. This issue may have been struck to commemorate a visit of the king to Seleucia, for it reminds us somewhat of the ADVENTUS AVGVSTI types of Roman coins.

After this issue the Parthian coins relapse into semi barbarity. The style becomes cruder and cruder, the types chosen are banal and usually badly executed, the inscriptions practically illegible and, on the drachms at least, repeated in meaningless fashion from reign to reign. The "portraits" grow ever more stereotyped, losing all pretense at achieving individual likenesses as between king and king—except in so far as some may be portrayed as bearded, others clean shaven. From a splendid beginning the Parthian coinage has finally degenerated until it has lost all claim to its proud Hellenic heritage.

SEVENTEEN

THE SUB-PARTHIAN
KINGDOMS

Persis

THE Parthian Empire was distinctly feudal in character, being composed of several large kingdoms whose rulers enjoyed considerable local independence but definitely acknowledged the Parthian king as their over-lord or suzerain. One of the largest and most powerful of these semi-independent kingdoms was Persis, the historic home of the Persians, whence sprang not only the famous line of the Achaemenid kings but also that of the no less famous Sassanians. Here there lived and ruled a long line of native kings throughout the five centuries which intervened between the death of Darius III and the great revolt in 228 A.D. which placed the princes of the Sassanian dynasty upon the throne of Iran. Yet nothing has been transmitted to us of their history, and even their names were absolutely unknown until after the middle of last century, when their coins began to appear on the market and learned scholars commenced, at first hesitatingly and painfully, to decipher their names one by one.

The earliest coins of the series, rare tetradrachms and drachms, bear the name of one Bagadat whose reign may be placed about 280 B.C. The obverse bears his bearded portrait, while on the reverse he is depicted either enthroned to l. (Fig. 1) or standing before a large fire altar. His immedi-

ate successors bore various names (deciphered as Oborzes, Artaxerxes I, Autophradates and the like) and

Figure 1.

Figure 2.

struck somewhat similar coins. The tetradrachm here illustrated (Fig. 2) is assigned to Autophradates. On the obverse we see this ruler's striking portrait, bearded, diademed and wearing the Persian "bashlik" or felt cap or hood; while on the reverse he stands in adoration before a crenelated Persian fire altar surmounted by the winged figure of the great god Ahura-Mazda. On the r. is depicted the sacred banner of the Persians which, like the Oriflamme of France, inspired and led their warriors to battle.

About the middle of the second century B.C. there came into power a ruler by the name of Darius I who, to judge by the extent of his issues (Fig. 3), must have enjoyed a long and prosperous reign. He struck tetra-

Figure 3.

drachms and drachms not unlike the preceding, but with an eagle surmounting his headdress and another eagle perched upon the standard on the reverse.

Figure 4.

Figure 5.

Darius' successor Autophradates II coined even more extensively, but henceforth only in drachms (Fig. 4) and their fractions. A crescent replaces the eagle on the obverse, while the design of the reverse has become greatly simplified. Towards the end of his reign he openly acknowledges Parthian suzerainty upon his coins by assimilating (Fig. 5) his portrait to that of Mithradates II. Only the continued presence of the crescent above his head serves to distinguish the portraits of the two rulers.

Autophradates' son Darius II follows with coins (Fig. 6) which on their obverses closely imitate the later issues of his suzerain Mithradates II. On their reverses the Persian king stands to left before an altar of Par-

Figure 6.

thian shape, while the accompanying inscription now boxes in the design as is the invariable practice on Parthian royal issues.

Figure 7.

Figure 8.

Artaxerxes II, son of Darius II, on his coins (Fig. 7) wears a crenelated crown. His brother Oxathres (Fig. 8) follows his contemporary Parthian over-lords (Orodes and Phraates IV) in wearing only the simple diadem. The succeeding Persian princes now commence to vary their reverse types, and under Piruz (or Pakur as the name is also read), son of Oxathres, we find a triskelis (Fig. 9), while his brother Namopat employs a star and crescent (Fig. 10) or depicts himself adoring this typically eastern symbol.

We have now reached the first quarter of the first Christian century, the point at which we brought to a close our description of the Parthian royal issues. The kings of Persis continued for two more centuries to issue coins, but with ever poorer style

Figure 9.

Figure 10.

and poverty of invention. Then gradually, towards the close of the second century, A.D., the style improves again, the flans become flatter and more spread, and we commence clearly to recognize that remarkable upward swing in the ability and originality shown by the die cutters which eventually resulted in the splendid and beautiful issues of the earlier sovereigns of the Sassanid dynasty.

Elymais

The province of Elymais, situated between Babylonia on the west and Persis on the east, was the heart of the old kingdom of Elam so frequently mentioned in the Bible. With its capital in the great city of Susa, Elymais was but a province under Seleucid rule. When that empire commenced seriously to weaken and to disintegrate in the course of the second century B.C., a native line of princes seems to have come into power. Of their history we know as little as we do of Persis — except that one of them, Kamnaskires, is mentioned by Lucian in his list of rulers who lived to a great old age.

Figure 11.

The first ruler known to have struck coins, Kamnaskires I Nikephoros, is represented only by rare tetradrachms and drachms. Of the next ruler, Kamnaskires and his queen Anzaze, numerous tetradrachms, drachms and minor fractions have survived. The royal pair is portrayed (Fig. 11) facing to left, decked in richly embroidered robes, the king with a broad diadem, the queen with necklace, diadem and a high, imposing coiffure. On the reverse of these coins is enthroned Zeus Nikephoros — who is probably the god Belus whose temple in Susiana Antiochus III attempted to despoil and was immediately punished by the god with death for the sacriligious act.

Other princes, all bearing the dynastic name of Kamnaskires, follow. They struck tetradrachms and drachms in ever poorer alloy. After Kamnaskires III the types remain invariably the same: on the obverse the bearded, diademed and richly robed bust of the king accompanied by the

Figure 12.

Seleucid anchor (?) surmounted by a star (Fig. 12) or star and crescent (Figs. 13, 14); on the reverse is a

Figure 13.

Figure 14.

smaller diademed and bearded head with a long inscription in debased Greek letters around. The final issues of the dynasty (Figs. 13, 14) are of pure copper, while the reverse type has become so barbarized that only a few meaningless strokes remain to do duty for diademed head and inscription!

The dynasty of the Kamnaskires came to an end in the first century A.D. and was followed by a group of princes bearing typically Parthian names, such as Phraates and Orodes. They struck prolific issues of copper tetradrachms and drachms, but these, because of their late date, are outside the time limits which we have set for our study.

Characene

The province of Characene comprised the plains and marshy lands in the delta of the Tigris and Euphrates rivers at the head of the Persian Gulf. When the rise of the Parthian kingdom at least partially blocked the overland trade routes between Syria, Central Asia and India, Characene rose rapidly in wealth and importance. In the second century B.C., during the final phases of the contest between the Seleucid and Parthian empires, Characene secured her independence under a line of local princes. But later these were constrained to acknowledge the suzerainty of the Parthian monarchs.

The first king, Hyspaosines, son of Sagdodonakos, refounded near the modern Mohammerah the old Alexandria (later Antiochia), first erected by Alexander and later destroyed by a devastating inundation. The new city was named Spasinou Charax after its founder, and soon attained great commercial importance as the place where the busy cross-desert trade route from Palmyra met the sea route from India and the East. Hyspaosines, as well as two of his successors, is known to us from Lucian as having attained to a ripe old age. He is further known by some rare tetradrachms and some over-struck

Figure 15.

[99]

copper pieces, the latter recently published by the present writer.

His successors, Apodakos, Tiraios, Attambelos I (Fig. 15), Theonisios, Adinerglos etc. (whose semitic and Iranian names sound as strange in our ears as their coins are rare in our cabinets) also issued tetradrachms and drachms. Fortunately they are invariably dated according to the Seleucid era so that the approximate dates of these kings can be more or less accurately determined. The types remain the same throughout. On the obverse we see the diademed portrait, usually bearded, of the king, while on the reverse Heracles is seated to left upon a rock resting his club on his right knee — similar to the coins of Antiochus II of Syria and Euthydemus I of Bactria. Like the contemporary coins of Elymais, those of Characene too, rapidly deteriorate both in their style and in the quality of their metal.

Figure 16.

It is not until the reign of Attambelos III, 53-71 A.D., that the coins (Fig. 16) become at all common. These tetradrachms are now quite crude in style and their metal is almost pure copper, sometimes washed with an extremely thin coating of silver. Similar coins of succeeding reigns are also known, but they are increasingly unattractive and also lie outside the limits set for our study.

EIGHTEEN

THE LATER KINGS
OF EGYPT

AFTER the death of Ptolemy I the Egyptian silver and copper coinages continue to reproduce his types in a uniform and monotonous manner throughout the remainder of the dynasty. Each issue is differentiated from its predecessor only by regnal dates, mint marks and increasingly poorer style. Here and there, however, like scattered but welcome oases in a vast Sahara, do we find refreshing instances of true portrait coinages.

Some ten years after he had ascended the Egyptian throne, Ptolemy II (285-246 B.C.) married his beautiful, masterful, ambitious and equally unscrupulous sister Arsinoe, formerly the wife of Lysimachus of Thrace. She immediately established an undoubted ascendancy over her clever but somewhat easy going brother, who, never the less, was intelligent enough to appreciate his sister's special abilities and allowed her powers their fullest scope. Arsinoe soon completely dominated her brother and was the real power behind the throne. When she died in 270/69 B.C. his grief was probably genuine enough. He raised her to the status of a goddess, established her worship throughout his dominions, inaugurated a new era dating from her death, and finally named a province (the modern Fayum) and many cities in her honor. He issued a splendid series of dated gold octodrachms (Fig. 1), silver decadrachms and tetradrachms bearing her portrait with sceptre, veil and diadem. A beautiful and imperious woman she must indeed have been, to judge by

Figure 1.

these handsome coins. Students and collectors have always called these gold coins "octodrachms"— but a recently discovered papyrus informs us that to the ancients they were known as Mnaeia (that is, a Mina) and so passed current for sixty Ptolemaic silver drachms.

Figure 2.

Barring some rare Arsinoe octodrachms struck in the Phoenician mints, only the silver decadrachms (Fig. 2) continued to be coined annually under Ptolemy II's successor

Figure 3.

Euergetes (246-221 B.C.). With them he issued gold octodrachms (Fig. 3) and tetradrachms (Mnaeia and half Mnaeia) bearing the combined portraits of his ancestors: the Savior Gods Ptolemy I and Berenice occupying the obverse, the Brother-and-Sister Gods, Ptolemy II and Arsinoe, occupying the reverse. The portraits of the older pair are typical likenesses drawn from their own issues; while the portrait of Ptolemy II well illustrates his personality as described by a modern historian (Bevan): "Ptolemy the son was a very different character from Ptolemy the father. The softening of fibre which became more pronounced in several later kings already showed itself in the son of the tough old Macedonian marshal. It was something of the contrast between David and Solomon, the magnificent voluptuary with intellectual and artistic interests succeeding the man of war. He (Ptolemy II) was of fair complexion, an obvious European, probably of a ruddy corpulence; there was plainly in the kings of this house an inherited tendency to grow fat in later life."

But Euergetes struck his own special coinages, too. In the first place there is an inspiring series of gold and

silver coins, issued in numerous denominations, in honor of his wife, the beautiful, brave and great souled

Figure 4.

Berenice II of Cyrene. Some of these coins, the gold decadrachms (Fig. 4), the silver dodecadrachm, are among the largest in these metals ever coined by the ancients. Like the constellation, Coma Berenices — named in her honor by an admiring courtier-astronomer — do these splendid coins glitter in our trays and ennoble by their presence the collections of their fortunate possessors. Her grave, beautiful, full cheeked countenance, set off by the graceful folds of her mantle, is indeed a pleasure to behold (Fig. 5).

Figure 5.

Her coins may not all be actually so rare as many another Ptolemaic issue, but they remain the finest in the series, and the constant demand by appreciative collectors has enhanced their market value enormously.

In the person of Ptolemy Euergetes there was once more a strong and war-like prince on the throne of Egypt. At the very outset of his reign he invaded Syria and secured "the greatest military triumph ever achieved by the house of Ptolemy." He seems indeed to have carried all before him. After subjugating Cilicia and northern Syria he moved across the Euphrates into Mesopotamia, possibly even into Persia, whence he brought back to Egypt the statues and divine images long ago removed thence by Persian conquerors. His fleets captured many cities dotted along the coasts of Asia Minor and Thrace.

Concerning the most important event in the campaign a tattered papyrus fragment gives us an extraordinarily vivid description, obviously written by an actual eye-witness, possibly even by the king himself. Such portions as can still be made out, read about as follows: "Meanwhile Pythagoras and Aristocles with 15 boats . . . sailed along the coast to Soli in Cilicia, where they collected the money which had been seized and deposited there and conveyed it to Seleucia (in Cilicia). It amounted to 1500 talents of silver. This money Aribazus the strategos in Cilicia (evidently a Persian in the Seleucid service) had intended to send to Ephesus, to Laodice (wife of Seleucus II), but the citizens of Soli had conspired with the soldiers, Pythagoras and Aristocles had come in strength to their assistance, and all had given a brave account of themselves — with the result that this

money had been seized and both the town and the citadel had fallen into our possession. Aribazus slipped out and got away as far as the pass over the Taurus; there certain of the natives cut off his head and brought it to Antioch. For our part, when we had got everything in readiness on board, at the beginning of the first watch we embarked in as many ships as the harbor in Seleucia would hold, and sailed along the coast to the fortress called Posideon (in Syria) and anchored there about the eighth hour of the day. Thence at dawn we set sail again and reached Seleucia (on the Orontes, in Syria). The priests, the magistrates, the rest of the citizens, the officers, and the soldiers met us on the road leading to the harbor, crowned with garlands . . . goodwill towards us . . . the sacrificial victims stationed beside . . . on the altars prepared by them. When they had outdone in the bazaar the honors already paid us they . . . so this day . . . and the next day. . . . The ships into which we took up all those who had sailed with us, and the satraps who were there, and the generals and the other officers, except those appointed (to garrison duty) in the city and the citadel, whom we left behind. (When we reached) Antioch . . . such preparations . . . we found as to strike us with amazement. For there came to meet us outside the gate the satraps and the other officers and the soldiers and the priests and the colleges of magistrates and all the young men from the gymnasium and a great multitude beside, crowned with garlands, and they carried out all the holy things (i.e. images of gods, etc.) into the road before the gate, and some greeted us with the right hand and others . . . with shouting and applause. . . . Though there were so many things (calculated to gratify us) nothing gave us so much pleasure as the intense loyalty of these people. When then we had sacrificed the victims presented to us by the officers and by private persons, the sun now verging to its decline, we immediately visited the Sister (Ptolemy's wife Berenice who had preceded him to Antioch), and after that attended to various matters which required our diligence, giving audience to the officers and the soldiers and to other people belonging to the place, and holding council on the general conduct of our affairs. Beside this for some days. . . ." Here breaks off, all too soon, one of the most extraordinary documents which the sands of Egypt have ever vouchsafed us — apparently the conquering king's own description of his triumphal entry into Seleucia, and then into Antioch, the capital of his Seleucid enemy!

Euergetes appears to have struck no coins at Antioch, though he did so elsewhere. Fortunately many of these coins bear portraits of himself, or of his wife Berenice. For instance, Fig. 6 shows a tetradrachm struck by him at Lebedus in Ionia, Fig. 7, another

Figure 8.

struck at Aenus in Thrace. The well known gold octodrachms (Fig. 8) which bear his portrait are mostly of Alexandrian mintage and were struck after his death. On these Euergetes plainly shows the corpulency to which his family was addicted, but that does not in the least detract from the impressiveness of his appearance. We see his fine profile, his royal air, the radiate crown which adorns his brow, the sacred aegis about his neck, the trident of Poseidon at his shoulder — all as behooved a great conqueror on land and sea.

Ancient historians agree in calling Ptolemy IV Philopator (221-203 B.C.), who succeeded, a sot and a soft voluptuary, under whose reign Egypt fell from a powerful and widely respected state to a condition of feebleness from which she never really recovered. Philopator, interested only in his own personal ease and the constant pursuit of pleasure, allowed his kingdom, as well as himself, to be run by a court cabal under the leadership of the clever but unscrupulous Sosibius — whom Polybius describes as

Figure 6.

Figure 7.

a "cunning and world-practised old scoundrel." The rare coins, gold octodrachms and silver tetradrachms,

Figure 9.

which give us the fourth Ptolemy's portrait, depict him as fat but still a rather good looking, self indulgent, self satisfied young man with sideburns. On many of his coins (Fig. 9) the initials ΣΩ of the unspeakable Sosibius also appear. Very rare octodrachms, together with some tiny copper coins, are known with the somewhat piquant features of Arsinoe III, Ptolemy's unhappy sister and wife. Most, if not all, of these coins were actually coined under his successor, Ptolemy V Epiphanes. Philopator himself died under very mysterious circumstances, and Justin claims that his death was kept secret for a long time by the court camarilla.

Be that as it may, it is certain that the unfortunate Arsinoe was soon after deliberately murdered. Polybius depicts an extraordinarily vivid scene of the public announcement made by the conspirators, the solemn crowning of Philopator's little child, the growing murmurs of the populace, the gradual spread of resentment at the dastardly murder, and eventually the popular explosion which swept the country and ended in the slaughter of all the conspirators.

Philip V of Macedon and Antiochus III of Syria now made a concerted move against Egypt's foreign posses-

sions. To the former fell all the Ptolemaic holdings in Thrace and Asia Minor; to the latter, Coele-Syria, Phoenicia and Palestine — finally sealed by the decisive battle of Panion (200 B.C.) which definitely forced Egypt back to within her own borders near the modern Suez Canal.

Figure 10.

From the very outset of Ptolemy V's reign gold octodrachms and silver tetradrachms (Fig. 10) were coined with the portrait of the young Epiphanes. Many of these bear mint marks, and we have issues, frequently dated, of Berytus, Byblus, Tripolis, Sidon, Tyre, Damascus, Ake and Joppa covering the few years just before these cities were captured by Antiochus III. Most attractive are these coins with the youthful and well modeled bust of Epiphanes on the obverse, the usual Ptolemaic eagle on the reverse. After the conclusion of the disastrous Syrian war, Egypt remained at peace with her neighbors, though it took some years to suppress completely the native rebellions which had been going on in Egypt itself for many years. Epiphanes, after he had grown up, had little chance to exhibit any possible military prowess, but his was a far more vigorous personality than that of his father. He devoted most of his time to hunting and athletic exercises. Certainly his portrait gives him a more up and doing air than that of his father. He married Cleopatra I, daughter of Antiochus III, and by her had three children, two boys and a girl, all of whom, for better or for worse, made their mark in Egyptian history. He died in 181 B.C. at the early age of twenty-eight.

Ptolemy VI Philometor, who now succeeded, unfortunately did not adopt his father's practice of placing his own portrait upon the coin of the realm. His silver issues merely repeat the long accustomed types of Ptolemy I; his gold (both octodrachms and tetradrachms), the types of Arsinoe II. The latter are distinguished from the earlier issues under Ptolemies II and III by their higher relief, poorer style, and by the very large K to be seen behind the veiled bust on the ob-

Figure 11.

verse (Fig. 11). As the features here vary somewhat from those of Arsinoe II, it has been supposed — possibly with some justice — that they were intended to portray Cleopatra I, Philometor's able mother who, for the eight years of his minority, acted as Queen-Regent of the kingdom.

Only one rare issue of tetradrachms is known to bear Philometor's own portrait. These were coined at Ake-Ptolemais in Palestine, whither he had gone to install his protegé, Alexander Bala, on the throne of Syria. It is a real pity that these coins should be so rare, because they furnish us

with a good portrait of one of the most attractive characters that ever reigned over Egypt. His was a most gentle and forgiving nature. Polybius says — and Polybius was in a position to know very well — that Ptolemy Philometor combined with his goodness and kindliness a presence of mind and high courage in perilous crisis and on the battlefield. Bevan says: "His diplomacy in regard to Rome was resolute and courageous, as well as skillful and urbane. He took personal part in more than one war, all of them carried to a successful close. . . . And he received his mortal hurt riding . . . amongst the fighters in the field, after the manner of the old Macedonian chiefs from whom he sprang."

In 145 B.C. there succeeded to the Egyptian throne Philometor's appalling brother (for his son Eupator had died before him) Ptolemy VIII, known as Euergetes II. In character he was an utter contrast to his excellent brother. His was a savage, vindictive, unscrupulous nature and he maintained his sway over Egypt for thirty odd years by banishments, confiscations of property, executions and massacres. He also appears to have achieved the distinction of becoming the fattest of all the Ptolemies and was popularly known by the nickname of Physcon or "pot belly." The anecdote is related that once the noted Roman, Aemilius Scipio, visited Alexandria with his friend Panaetius of Rhodes. The mountainous Euergetes came down to the landing place to greet his distinguished guest and then, puffing and panting, escorted him on foot from the ship to the palace. "The

Alexandrians" whispered Scipio to Panaetius "owe me one thing; they have at last seen their king walk!"

Figure 12.

The only known portrait which we possess of this monstrosity is to be found on some extremely rare didrachms (Fig. 12) struck at Alexandria in 138/7 B.C. The die cutter must surely have seen the king in person, for he gives us a most convincing portrayal of Euergetes II, with bloated cheeks, protruding eye, and flaring nostril — the living picture of an abnormally fat man suffering from asthma.

As no more portrait coins appear until the second reign (54-51 B.C.) of Ptolemy XIII Auletes, the "Fluteplayer," we need not delay over the intervening kings. They all, including Auletes, continued year after year to coin with the familiar and now completely stereotyped types of Ptolemy I. Auletes, who seems never to have been very popular with his subjects, was eventually forced to flee the country in 58 B.C. In 55 B.C. he returned with the help of Aulus Gabinius, proconsul of Asia, who with an army invaded Egypt and replaced Auletes on the throne. In the second year after

his restoration (the twenty-eighth of his reign) he struck a few drachms (Fig. 13) bearing his portrait — a strange profile—with protruding nose and bushy hair over the brow.

And now we come to the last Greek sovereign of Egypt, the famous and inimitable Cleopatra. Oldest child of Auletes, she far surpassed her spendthrift father in strength of character, ability and cleverness. For twenty years she ruled Egypt with a firm hand, successfully contending against the intrigues of her sister and brothers, as well as the covetousness of Rome, steering her ship between the rocks and eddies of the mighty civil wars which split the western world from end to end — until finally Octavian emerged supreme ruler of the Roman State and determined to add Egpyt to its dependencies. Then at last Cleopatra despaired and bravely died by her own hand rather than grace the triumph of Caesar's nephew. Only a Shakespeare or a Plutarch can do her full justice — though many an able writer has tried his hand — and books dealing with her fascinating story have appeared in countless numbers, and doubtless will ever continue to appear, for:
"Age cannot wither her, nor custom Stale her infinite variety."

In addition to some portrait drachms which, in imitation of her father, she struck in her sixth year,

Figure 13.

Figure 14.

she also issued a prolific series of copper coins in two denominations. The larger (Fig. 14) bears the value mark Π, the smaller Μ— indicating that these pieces represented eighty and forty copper drachms respectively. So low, by this time, had the Egyptian copper currency fallen. The reverse type is the usual Ptolemaic eagle, the obverse Cleopatra's diademed portrait.

To one who knows only the Cleopatras of stage, screen and popular fancy, her strong and almost forbidding features come as a distinct shock. But Plutarch definitely says: "For her beauty . . . was in itself not altogether incomparable, nor such as to strike those who saw her; but converse with her had an irresistible charm, and her presence, combined with the persuasiveness of her discourse and the character which was somehow diffused about her behaviour towards others, had something stimulating about it."

We may place complete confidence in the general accuracy of these Egyptian coin portraits, for were they not executed at Alexandria where die-cutters had ample opportunity to behold the queen? Had not a long tradition of splendid and life-like portrayals of the sovereigns always characterized the Alexandrian coinage? Surely too, Cleopatra must have possessed both ordinary feminine and royal vanity, and would hardly have suffered a caricature to deface her coinage. Lastly, her features, as portrayed on the Egyptian coins, are fully corroborated by her other portraits appearing on the tetradrachms and denarii struck at Antioch by Marc Antony, on her silver coinages of Ascalon, as well as on the numerous copper coins issued by the municipalities of Berytus, Damascus and Patras.

NINETEEN

HIERO II AND
HIS FAMILY

THE many powerful and famous tyrants, who from time to time ruled over the wealthy city of Syracuse in the fifth and fourth centuries B.C., were scrupulously careful to observe republican forms on the coinages issued under their rule. Agathocles (317-289 B.C.) was the first to strike money in his own name, but even he did not quite dare to take the final step of placing his likeness upon the coins — intensely interesting to us moderns as such a proceeding would have been. In fact, it was not until well on in the reign of the great Hiero II that the people's favor toward their ruler was felt to be so established that the precedent long since set by eastern Greek sovereigns was finally followed at Syracuse, and an interesting series of living portraits appear upon the city's coinages.

But Hiero II was a very exceptional man. No Greek tyrant ever succeeded quite so thoroughly in binding his people to himself. Indeed it is practically impossible to name another city-tyrant in all Greek history who reigned so long or so happily, and who retained his subjects' love and regard until the very day of his death. Neither do we read of another tyrant who ruled so wisely, so self effacingly, so continuously mindful of his country's best interests as did Hiero. Surely because of this fact he and his family are the first and only persons

ever openly to be portrayed upon Syracusan money.

From the very day of his birth, so the popular stories go, did the gods smile upon their protégé and show clearly, by oft repeated signs and wonders, the predestined greatness of an otherwise ordinary Syracusan citizen. As a young man Hiero did his duty in the army, and by his courage and pleasing personality won all hearts. When Pyrrhus finally left the Sicilian shores, factional strifes again broke out in Syracuse. The army revolted and chose as leaders Hiero and a certain Artemidorus. The soldiery forced an entry into the city and soon secured the upper hand. At once Hiero stepped to the front, won over the citizenry as he had the army, and ruled alone in Syracuse. His youth, his good looks, his brilliant talents, his wise statesmanship and, above all, his kindly disposition and benevolent rule firmly established him in the popular esteem. Hiero next proceeded to attach the aristocracy to his cause by marrying the beautiful and noble Philistis, daughter of a wealthy citizen, Leptines by name, descended from that Leptines who was a brother of the famous tyrant Dionysius the Elder.

Having now nothing to fear at home, Hiero next advanced against the Mamertines, a warlike people who had but recently crossed over from Italy. They had seized the city of

Messana and from there were gradually spreading out over the entire north-eastern corner of the island. In a well planned and brilliantly executed campaign he captured their outlying strongholds, freed the towns of Halaesa, Abacaenum and Tyndaris, utterly routed the Mamertine army in a pitched battle near their capital, and all but captured Messana itself — which was only saved, at the last moment, by the intervention of the Carthaginian fleet. But Hiero had won his spurs, and on his return home was given an ovation and hailed king of Syracuse by public acclaim (269 B.C.).

But soon the shadow of Rome falls upon the scene. Having finally driven Pyrrhus ignominiously out of Italy and subjected almost the entire Peninsula to her rule, Rome commenced to seek a foothold in the rich and fertile island of Sicily. The request for help now made to her by the Mamertines was gladly granted, and in 264 B.C. a Roman consul suddenly crossed the straits and occupied Messana. Both the Carthaginian and the Syracusan forces moved against the Romans, but with little actual cooperation between them. The Romans first attacked Hiero, who though successful with his cavalry was forced to retire with his foot soldiery. Thinking better of the entire political and military situation, he retreated the following day to Syracuse, and not long afterward made his peace with Rome. The treaty which followed recognized and respected his rule over Syracuse and the surrounding country, while the king on his side became an ally of Rome. And right loyally did Hiero stand by this treaty throughout the remainder of his long life.

While the ensuing First Punic War raged far and wide over and around the island, Hiero's little kingdom remained untouched. He himself, time and again, came to the aid of his Roman friends with corn, money and ships. Cleverly did he, for over fifty years, steer his ship of state through the rough and dangerous waters between the Roman Scylla and the Carthaginian Carybdis. No less wisely did he bestow every care upon the moral, intellectual and material advancement of his beloved Syracuse. Especially did he foster both commercial and agricultural activities, and maintain the closest contact with wealthy kingdoms such as Egypt, and successful business centres such as Rhodes. Syracuse became wealthy once more, her trading ships were to be found in all the principal Mediterranean ports. Large consignments of grain from her rich fields were sent either to aid her Roman allies or to relieve distress in Egypt. Rhodes was given a hundred talents (over two hundred thousand dollars) in cash, many costly vessels for the temples, and engines for rebuilding after a devastating earthquake had leveled alike temples, homes and even the world famous Colossus. The greatest poets and scholars of the age were enticed to the Syracusan court, on which such men as Bion, Theocritus and Archimedes shed undying lustre.

When Hiero was already over ninety years of age, the Second Punic War broke out. His favorite son, the heir presumptive Gelon, favored the Carthaginian cause; but the wise old king never faltered in his faith to Rome. He sent that city, in the dark days after the disaster at Lake Trasimene, a thousand slingers and archers, seventy-five thousand bushels of wheat, fifty thousand of barley, and a golden statue of Victory weighing three hundred and twenty pounds. Soon, however, intense grief overwhelmed Hiero at the sudden death of Gelon, and this loss he himself could not long survive. In 215 B.C. there passed away a truly great man, deeply mourned by his devoted people.

Well worthy the revived wealth and importance of Syracuse, and the greatness of her ruler, is the splendid series of coins which was issued during the latter half of Hiero's reign. This coinage was based on the local Sicilian silver litra, but so arranged as to fit in with the widespread coinage of the friendly kingdom of Ptolemaic Egypt. The style and general character of the coinage also follows Egyptian models. The largest silver coin is an impressive thirty-two litra piece, bearing on its obverse a fine, diademed portrait of Hiero, while a stately quadriga, guided by a winged Victory, fills the reverse field. The sixteen litra piece, the equivalent of a Ptolemaic tetradrachm, has the same reverse type (sometimes the quadriga is depicted as in full gallop), while the obverse is graced by the lovely veiled head of the noble Philistis, in the guise

also known, bearing similar types but with a biga replacing the quadriga because of the smaller flan (Fig. 2).

Figure 2.

Figure 3.

Figure 4.

Accompanying these are also eight (Fig. 3) and four litra (Fig. 4) pieces, with the youthful Gelon's portrait, in whose features may be recognized striking similarities to both his father and his mother. The large silver denomination, with the portrait of Hiero, is extremely rare. But, fortunately for collectors, there exists a plentiful series of handsome bronze coins

Figure 1.

of Demeter (Fig. 1). Five litra pieces — equal to the Attic drachm — are

Figure 5.

(Fig. 5) fully equal to the silver coins in style, which give us both laureate and diademed heads of Hiero. Their reverses have for type an armed warrior astride a prancing steed.

Upon Hiero's death his second son, Hieronymus, ascended the throne. He was a youth of but fifteen years of age, the complete antithesis of his father, and completely spoiled into the bargain. Wise counsellors were left to guide him, but these were soon ousted by the selfish intrigues of the courtiers, who, themselves soon came to grief under the whims and displeasures of the foolish young tyrant. To cap the climax, Hieronymus now made overtures to Carthage and commenced to war against the Roman possessions in Sicily. A conspiracy was set on foot, Hieronymus was enticed to Leontini, separated from his bodyguard and assassinated. Thereupon all was confusion, irresolution and internecine strife. The Roman fleet appeared before Syracuse, and eventually an army, under the great Marcellus, commenced the memorable siege of the city. It ended in 212 B.C. with the fall and sack of Syracuse, the death of her noted citizen, Archimedes, and her own final subjection to Roman rule.

In spite of his very short reign, many of the coins of the young Hiero-

Figure 6.

Figure 7.

nymus are far from rare. Ten (Fig. 6) and five (Fig. 7) litra pieces in silver, together with the accompanying bronze coins — all bearing his portrait — are to be had without great difficulty. His features, fat, stupid, self-indulgent and rather ignoble, proclaim his character only too well, and offer sad commentary on the frequent failure of transmission of virtues from father to son.

TWENTY

THE KINGS OF NUMIDIA
AND MAURETANIA

THE kings of Numidia first come into historical prominence towards the
close of the Second Punic War. Numidia was at that time divided into
an eastern and a western portion, respectively ruled by Gula and Syphax.
The former, residing at Cirta (the
modern Constantine), sided with Carthage, the latter with Rome.

After years of internecine warfare
between these kings and their successors, Massinissa, son of Gula, finally gained the upper hand. A man
praised by ancient writers for his
courage, vigor, perseverance, and fru-
gality, he possessed an insatiable desire for power and glory. He formed
a powerful kingdom which, on his
death in 148 B.C., was left to his son
Micipsa. To Massinissa many coins
in all metals have been assigned, but
the only ones certainly his consist of

Figure 1.

a prolific series of bronze coins (Fig.
1) bearing a laureate, bearded and
strong-featured portrait on the obverse and a galloping horse, accompanied by a pellet or by initial letters
in Punic, on the reverse.

Micipsa, great friend of the Ro-

mans and their able ally in many campaigns, enjoyed a long and, on the
whole, prosperous reign. He was well
educated, cultivated the sciences, especially philosophy, and enhanced the
well being and wealth of his kingdom
until his death in 118 B.C. He continued the issues of his father, but
they are of somewhat poorer style and
on their reverses bear a walking horse,

Figure 2.

accompanied by various symbols and
letters (Fig. 2).

On his death, the kingdom was divided between his sons Adherbal and
Hiempsal I and his adopted son Jugurtha. The latter was far and away
the most able and aggressive of the
three, and by 112 B.C. had disposed
of his rivals and secured the entire
kingdom. War soon broke out with
Rome, which lasted off and on for six
years. The forces of the Republic were
time and again worsted by Jugurtha,
and it eventually took the generalship
of a Metellus, followed by that of the
redoubtable Marius himself, to overcome the desperate courage and wily
ability of the Numidian king. Jugurtha was taken to Rome in 106 B.C.

and two years later was forced to walk with his two sons before the triumphal chariot of Marius. He died soon after, in prison.

Figure 3.

Certain silver didrachms (Fig. 3) and drachms have been assigned, with some show of reason but little certainty, to Jugurtha. Their obverses bear a laureate, clean-shaven portrait head with strikingly individual features. On the reverse is an elephant, an animal which constituted a major part of Jugurtha's military power.

Next Hiempsal II (circa 106-60 B.C.) became king of a small portion of Numidia. Little is known of his history except that for a time in 88 B.C. his kingdom was a refuge for Marius and in 81 B.C. he was driven from his kingdom by one Hiarbas. Sulla sent Pompey to Africa to reinstate Hiempsal, who thereafter ruled peacefully until his death about 60 B.C. Like many of his predecessors he was a cultivated man, and is even said, by Sallust, to have written a history of Numidia.

To Hiempsal II have been assigned

Figure 4.

some silver denarii (Fig. 4), quinarii and sestertii bearing a beardless male head, crowned with wheat ears, on the obverse, and a galloping horse in a wreath or circle on the reverse. The attribution is possible, though still highly conjectural.

Juba I succeeded his father about 60 B.C. During the Civil Wars he joined the Pompeian party and in 49 B.C. attacked Caesar's lieutenant Curio near Utica and annihilated both commander and army. In 47 B.C. Juba united his forces with the Pompeians under Scipio and together they met Caesar at the famous battle of Thapsus which ended in their utter defeat. The following year Juba committed suicide.

Figure 5.

His interesting denarii (Fig. 5) portray the king with robe, sceptre and diadem, his long beard and hair carefully arranged and curled. This reminds us of Cicero's characterization of the king, when he first came to Rome, as *adolescens bene capillatus*; while Suetonius relates that once, in an interview, he so enraged Caesar that the latter completely lost control of himself and seized the king by his beard! On Juba's death his kingdom was incorporated with the Roman province of Africa.

The Kings of Western Numidia

The great rival of Gula and Massinissa was Syphax who ruled over western Numidia, now Algeria, with his capital at Siga, just west of the modern Oran. At first the friend of the Romans and of Scipio, Syphax was eventually won over to the Carthaginian side, perhaps less by the arguments of Hasdrubla than by the charms of the latter's beautiful daughter Sophonisba who was offered to Syphax in marriage. When Scipio finally landed in Africa in 204 B.C., Syphax joined the Carthaginians with an army of sixty thousand men. The following year Scipio made an attack, as sudden as it was brilliant, and practically annihilated the Numidian army, as well as that of their Carthaginian allies. Twice more was Syphax defeated by the Romans and eventually fell into their hands. According to Polybius he was taken to Rome and lived to adorn the triumph of Scipio, dying shortly afterwards.

Figure 6.

Rare bronze coins (Fig. 6) have been attributed to Syphax which bear the king's diademed and bearded head on the obverse and a galloping horseman (the pride and strength of the Numidian armies) on the reverse. Similar coins are also known of Vermina, the son of Syphax, except that in this case the portrait is beardless and faces to the right, while a galloping horse replaces the horseman of his father's coins.

The Kings of Mauretania

Practically nothing is known of the early history of Mauretania. In the second and first centuries B.C. we hear of several kings named Bocchus and Bogud, some of whom struck coins but frequently without por-

Figure 7.

traits. Fig. 7 is a bronze coin of Bocchus, probably the last of the line. He was recognized as king by Caesar in 49 B.C. and was his ally in the war against Juba I. He later sided with Octavian and died in 33 B.C.

In the meanwhile the son of Juba I, also named Juba, was taken to Rome by Caesar, adorned his triumph, and was given a careful education in the Dictator's own family. He was a playmate of the little Octavian, grew up to be his staunch friend and took part in the battle of Actium. Augustus gave him the hand of Cleopatra Selene (daughter of Marc Antony and the great Cleopatra), and, in 25 B.C., established him as king of Mauretania. He resided at Iol, which he renamed Caesarea (the modern Cherchel) in honor of the emperor, and embellished this city with splendid buildings and beautiful statuary. He carried out several important geographical expeditions and wrote numerous valuable works on geography and history which were later much quoted from by Pliny, Plutarch and Athenaeus.

Throughout his long and prosperous reign of forty-eight years Juba II struck large numbers of denarii and bronze coins, frequently dated and bearing numerous interesting types.

Many of these reverse types are in honor of Cleopatra and so allude to Egypt or the Egyptian religion (the sacred cow of Hathor, crocodile, sym-

Figure 8.

Figure 9.

Figure 10.

bols of Isis, sitrum etc., Figs. 8, 9, 10), while others celebrate Juba's victories and the triumphal honors decreed to him by the Senate. Yet others refer to the sacred grove (Fig. 11), altars,

Figure 11.

Figure 12.

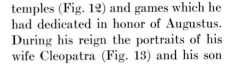

temples (Fig. 12) and games which he had dedicated in honor of Augustus. During his reign the portraits of his wife Cleopatra (Fig. 13) and his son

Figure 13.

Figure 14.

Ptolemy (Fig. 14) also adorn the coins. Juba II died about 23-4 A.D. and was succeeded by Ptolemy who reigned until his assassination by order of the mad Caligula in 40 A.D. He too struck a prolific series of denarii and copper coins, whose types, however, are mostly borrowed from Juba's issues. Ptolemy at times introduced a

Figure 15.

few new types such as palm tree (Fig. 15), caduceus, wheat ears, and the like. On his death Mauretania was incorporated as a Roman province, thus bringing to an end the long and at times interesting series of coins issued by the Numidian and Mauretanian kings.

INDEX
OF
KINGS

INDEX OF KINGS

INDEX OF KINGS

INDEX OF KINGS

INDEX OF KINGS

INDEX OF KINGS

INDEX OF KINGS

INDEX OF KINGS

INDEX OF KINGS

NOTES

NOTES

NOTES